Barbara and Elizabeth

Late-Life Lovers

Elizabeth F. Boardman

meetinghouse
newberg, or 97132

Barbara and Elizabeth
Late-Life Lovers

©2022 by Elizabeth F. Boardman

Meetinghouse
Newberg, Oregon
https://www.meetinghouse.xyz/

Printed in the United States of America

Cover and page design by Mareesa Fawver Moss

Cover art by Darryl Brown

ISBN 978-1-59498-091-6

For my three sisters
and the other wonderful women
who have shared the road
so far

Table of Contents

Table of Contents

1. Here we are

I love another woman, but I am not a lesbian. Barbara and I have grown and aged beyond the binary concepts of gay or straight. Maybe androgynous is the word for us.

We are "giving ourselves away" with this book in two senses. For starters, we are revealing many of our secrets, perhaps being more forthright than two women together have previously felt they could be.

We are also giving away to our readers the best of what we have learned about love and marriage during the first year together. Our experience may relate to yours, especially if you are a baby-boomer or even if you are somewhat younger. In many ways, one romance is like every other; isn't that true?

The story

Barbara Benham Tye and I fell in love, out of the blue, when we were both seventy-six years old. Our late-life romance was astounding to us, coming at a stage when neither of us needed or sought a liaison and certainly not with another woman. It has given us new perspectives on falling in love, sexuality, aging, and marriage that we want to share with others.

I, Elizabeth, am what might be called a compulsive writer. (This is my ninth book. Perhaps I write because I don't dare speak up in person. I am usually unwilling to ask for much attention face to face. Or maybe I'm afraid of in-person rejection.)

So I did the writing. But Barbara played an equally important role by suggesting topics, supporting the process, then repeatedly editing draft after draft. Sometimes the material included ideas we had not discussed previously so that our communication was enhanced and our relationship grew along with the writing project.

The contents

In the early intoxicated days of our romance, we were eager to find and write poems that put words to what we were feeling. Finding good poems wasn't easy, so we also wrote some ourselves.

We also went on a search for useful books about late-life love and attraction between women. The best of those are described in chapter 14.

I wondered if some of our "give-away" of sexual secrets was too explicit. But Barbara always supported the goal of being open and clear. We ourselves had looked for places to learn about loving sexual behavior, so others—especially curious women in their fifties and sixties—would probably be looking for this kind of thing, too. We are not much different from other people, gay or straight, young or old. So we figured we might as well tell it like it is. Except, of course, for those secrets we will never tell anyone.

The two of us

We are just ordinary women. We are fortunate to be educated, professional, generally successful, glad to be still alive and in more or less good health. We live in separate apartments in a pretty, small California retirement community which has attracted a marvelous assortment of lively, liberal, and cooperative people.

Barbara traveled around the world before and after marrying a colleague in the education department of a small university. Over the years there, he and then she served as chair of the department. They were greatly respected for their work in organization development, educational change, and K-12 global education. In addition, Barbara helped to raise Ken's children and is an active grandmother to the five children in the next generation. She was widowed, after thirty-five years of marriage, just two years before she and I met.

Meanwhile, I lived in San Francisco and worked with ailing elders in impoverished neighborhoods there for most of my professional life. My vocation was to develop and manage supportive housing and daytime care programs in the Tenderloin and South of Market neighborhoods. The mission was to help disabled old people to live in their own homes as long as possible.

On the personal side, I raised four children through challenging times. The family experience included mixed-race adoption, mental illness, teen pregnancy, alcoholism, physical violence, autism, and a divorce after sixteen years. We are real survivors. I have seven grandchildren.

Barbara and I are ordinary-looking women. I am a little taller than Barb; she a little heavier than I. We talk a lot, laugh a lot, share liberal political ideas and solid humanitarian values. We are both active in contributing to the life of the community we live in. Each of us suffers several minor health problems, but neither has anything fatal yet. We consider ourselves the luckiest people around and are deeply grateful for our good fortune.

Now the question is whether, still enthralled and in love with Barbara Benham Tye, will I be able to pull myself together enough to write something coherent about our experience? *Will I have the time and focus?*

Will we dare to have you read it? Well, let's try it and see. One step at a time!

Acknowledgments

Barbara could just as well have been listed as co-author of this book, but she prefers to be known as one of the two lead characters and acclaimed as a good editor and writing companion. Of course, I could not have lived this story, let alone written it, without her.

Even though Barbara and I do not experience ourselves as lesbians, others may see us that way. We are fully aware that our warm reception as a couple by family, friends, church, and community has been possible only because of the hard personal experiences and devoted advocacy efforts of many LGBT people over the past fifty years. We thank them from our hearts.

Several dear friends read early drafts of these pages with a red pencil in hand, an invaluable service. Many thanks to Faith Childs, Henrietta Cosentino, Valerie Kelsay, Karen Rose, Susan Sides, Marlane Spillinger, and Gloria Valoris. Some of you have marked up my manuscripts before; surely there will not be many others after this!

2. How it started

When I began writing about all this on April 7, 2018, trying to figure out what had hit me, Barb said it had started months before, as she got to know me and then began to get increasingly involved emotionally.

I thought of it as starting when we went together (her journal shows that was January 13) to see the movie *Call Me By Your Name*. Afterward, as we walked away through the parking lot, I took her arm, an innocent initiative on my part, and said something cavalier about young love. Barbara said, in a laden voice, "Such love is not always young."

Well, I got the picture right away that she was smitten. Having fallen for a guy or two in my time and having some experience with such emotions, I thought I would give her a chance to speak her mind (heart), and then she would get over it. So I did; but she didn't. Instead, she temporized, agreed to keep calm, and just to be a friend. We began to meet more often and to talk at greater depth.

As it happened, I had just come through a traumatic experience in a volunteer position I had held, so I was in a fragile and vulnerable state of mind. Barbara helped me think through how to deal with the situation and eventually to withdraw. (I remember I resigned on February 8.) I think it was when I had resolved that dilemma that I began to think about Barbara differently.

It might have been February 21 when I set up my convertible couch so that we could talk face to face with our legs slightly tangled together. But she sat facing forward in the conventional way. I threw my legs across her lap, and she gently fell over sideways into my arms. Except for the concept of "contact comfort," I don't remember a single thing about what we said or did that night or the next several days; shock put everything into a blur for me. We started writing notes and e-messages to one another about physical responses. Barbara became increasingly explicit. I was mind-blown—and increasingly excited. Here is one bit she wrote to me by e-mail.

> I hope you won't be shocked when I confess that one thing I did this afternoon was to go online and Google ways that women can please each other (or words to that effect). Lots of sites, some more helpful than others. I don't think I'll need to do that again, though, because what I got from it all was basically common sense. 1. Take it slow; 2. Don't let orgasm be the primary goal—enjoy

the journey; 3. Speak up; let each other know what you want/like (and don't want/like); 4. Follow your heart and your body's reactions; 5. Enjoy yourselves. When I add to that what you said in your spiritual journey presentation about letting go of self-consciousness (which, I admit, will be difficult for me), I feel ready for what may come. No pun intended.

It blew my socks off! Clearly, she was planning to make love with me sometime soon!

One of my sisters was scheduled to come to California that week. I went to Davis on the 27th to fetch her and was busy with her for days. She went to another relative overnight on March 2, so on that night, for the first time as I recollect it, I lay down with Barbara Benham Tye. No way was mere "contact comfort" enough for us!

My sister came back the next day. Barb and I gave a little wine and cheese party for her. We played it very cool, revealing nothing to anyone, and she left town the following day.

For the next month, Barbara and I were deeply ensconced in discovery and ecstasy, writing e-mail love notes constantly, exchanging cards and poems, meeting daily, lying together often at her place or mine. (Hers had a better bed; mine had a discreet back door.)

We were both astounded that this was happening at all because of our thoroughly heterosexual backgrounds, our age (seventy-six), and our less than perfect bodies. Barbara seemed to take it all in stride more easily than I did. I was "depraved on account I'm deprived," as the ruffians in *West Side Story* say. After twenty-three years of deliberate celibacy, loving, physical contact almost overwhelmed me. For those first few weeks, I was shocked, disoriented, scared, and practically out of control. *Can this really be me?!* Barbara, widowed only three years and married to a good man for thirty-five years before that, was less stunned and was patient with me.

During the liberal, feminist decades of the eighties and nineties, when considering the option of engaging romantically with a woman, I had always turned away from that possibility. I figured I would be as responsive to a woman's touch as to a man's, but I thought I would not be inclined to reciprocate, which would hardly be fair to the other woman. But now, with Barbara, ALL I could think about was how best to make love to her. Having conventional American ideas about feminine beauty, I had never imagined I would be attracted to a large woman, but now it was clear to me that ONLY a woman of her build could attract me.

We both started off saying that we wouldn't know what to do in bed, but then, of course, we did, exploring, guiding one another, moving through gentle trial and error, over and over. We lay entwined in every possible way, stroking and caressing and kissing for hours. This activity had nothing to do with "fucking," but was all about making love. It was the six-letter words that fit for us now: stroke, fondle, caress. Sometimes press and wrestle. For a few days there, I was stroking the side of the refrigerator or my computer desk if Barbara wasn't nearby for me to touch!

At first we worried, me especially, about being found out, about how to be discreet and mostly invisible to the dense community around us. But we moved petty steadily toward not worrying about it much. We transitioned from feeling guilty or defiant (me mostly) toward being easy and confident (her mostly). Slowly we decided whom to tell (long-distance friends at first, people who lived away from our retirement community), what to tell, and how.

We talked interminably about what we liked, knew, feared, imagined, wanted, promised, and could bring to the relationship. Increasingly we appreciated what a good match we were, our complementary strengths, our growing commitment, and especially our good luck. Neither of us had looked for such a romance or felt any need for it. Others who yearned for such a connection weren't making it. It wasn't fair.

A basic contract was already in place to undergird our growing relationship. Both of us were already committed to living as active members of this community until the end of our days. The setup was perfect. We each had an apartment that fit our needs and expressed our tastes. Our places were only 150 steps apart (170 if you went the back way to be discreet), so visiting one another was easy. We didn't have to deal with driving anywhere for our trysts. No searching for parking places! We were not under pressure to move away or to move in together in order to pursue a long-term commitment.

We did start to think about the long term immediately, which perplexed me—I hadn't done that at all during earlier romances with men. Was this a sudden reversion to conventional thinking? Was this some kind of old-lady assumption? Or had I just suddenly recognized Barbara as the independent, full-fledged, grown-up partner I had been looking for all my life? YES!

Do you know that it is a hardship as well as a blessing to be intelligent, energetic, independent, and competent, as well as being good-humored and kind? These words apply to me! That is a bold and brazen thing to say, isn't it? Now get this: Barbara Benham Tye is my equal in these traits, at the very least, as no man I've known intimately has ever been. She's the one I was looking for! I thought it would be a man.

I was worried that wistful flashbacks to her married days might assail Barbara now. But she was very clear that she was not inclined to look back. Her husband was a great guy, her long marriage was successful, and his death under her care was fully resolved. We would have his full blessing now, she was sure. She characterized herself as a person who lives wholeheartedly in the present.

Hours of bliss in bed and of joy in daily life became common for us. Yet moments of panic still arrived at a similar rate. There was still the shock of finding yourself engaged in a relationship you never remotely imagined and certainly never hoped for. An identity crisis. *Is this me, doing these things with another woman?*

Once or twice, struggling with this kind of panic myself, I projected it onto Barbara. When she left a phone message that I should not come to her because she had a new, contagious cold, I felt rejected and leapt to a different theory about what was going on. I began to assume the worst and to plan how I would survive without her. Fortunately, we were able to talk it out very soon.

My mind was in such a swirl. I kept stammering all the time. I would make strong declarative remarks— and then the next day change my mind. Barb didn't know what to expect.

> How beyond imagining wonder full
> that I should be blessed with your yes
> when it might well have been your no, so sorry.

There was a point of no return somewhere along the way when wildly excited infatuation deepened into confidence that this would last. I think it may have been the day Barbara told me without prior discussion, decisive woman that she is, that she had ordered a double bed to replace the single one she had bought only a year previous. It was a necessary investment in our relationship, she had concluded. I was astounded and delighted.

In the early days of sorting out, I sometimes dreamed in one way or another about men's bodies and male sexuality. But it was not worrisome. It seemed clear that my subconscious was doing the same work my conscious mind was doing: grappling with how a life-long straight woman who loved men's bodies could now be going with a woman.

I had a bad dream several nights running that featured two small planes dropping bombs and then flying in low overhead, strafing the village where I lived with my children. But the bombs were duds, and the bullets never seemed to hit anyone. Finally, before bed one night, I got out my favorite dream book to learn how I might interpret this recurring dream. Though I fell asleep without reading more than a page or two, in the morning I understood immediately that my subconscious was feeling under attack from two small, swift, powerful sources (Barb and myself), that I was "being bombed" by a barrage of alarming new ideas and facts, but that in the end, no one would get hurt. Once clarified, I never had that dream again.

Barbara's subconscious was worried, too, producing a dream about taking an exam and not being ready:

> The door opens, and we file in,
> take our assigned seats,
> place our number two pencils just so,
> and listen to the proctor politely,
> me hoping that our teacher wasn't
> just blowing steam
> the day he told us, "Don't worry, kids.
> When you need it, it will all be
> there in your heads."
> Me trusting that I will be
> able to give the right answers—
> a moment of panic; then
> I open my packet
> and begin.

I had a great time interpreting this dream, how it connects with us. But I didn't tell Barbara what I saw in it because she doesn't like analyzing dreams. Anyway, all such dreams faded away as we came to know one another and trust ourselves better.

Our main worry was that we had made an increasingly public commitment without really knowing whether we would be able to live it out. Of course, there is a shadow side to our future. One of us will die before the other, within a decade or two, possibly after a lingering illness and decline. It is scary to face this future when you are first falling in love. But it also adds a gratifying depth and substance to the relationship. So far, only one of us at a time seems to get overwhelmed and afraid so that the other can reassure her as needed.

The community of like-minded people around us supports our strong resolution to work through any problems we encounter. If our relationship were to weaken, it would mean only that we would spend less time together, each still in her own place and her own life. Also, we know the one who survives the other will be surrounded by a caring community and will still have ways to be useful to others.

3. Rules for ourselves

From the very beginning, we started putting together some rules for ourselves. The very first one, practically the first day, was from me: No perfume. How brazen to demand such a sudden change from a woman who has enjoyed fragrances! It's a wonder I didn't lose her on the spot. But I am super-sensitive to non-natural fragrances and simply can't breathe when near them. So this was non-negotiable.

I also asked for no lipstick, mostly so I could kiss her unrestrainedly without getting smudged up myself. But also, I don't much like how lipstick often looks. I think we should use so little, of a natural hue, that you can't tell we have it on but just think we look healthy and vibrant. This was also a big demand, I think, but Barb adhered to it without exception for many months.

Even now, it is only when she wears a red top and we won't be smooching in the next couple of hours that she will use a little color on her mouth.

We never had to ban long fingernails since neither of us had them, but we have talked about keeping nails clean, short, and smooth, given the ways we use our hands with one another.

We made more substantive rules as the time went on.

- No self-deprecation. American women are very prone to saying negative things about their own bodies, their cooking, their interior decor, and themselves, from a lack of self-esteem or to maneuver the listener into offering reassurance, even if it is false. We are really strict about not allowing derogatory comments of this sort between ourselves.

- No kissing in public, lest we make others uncomfortable. Even inside, at home, especially after dark, we draw the shades over our big windows before kissing and embracing.

- No holding hands or tangling legs during meetings and gatherings unless it's a movie and the lights are down. Even then, we sit in back rows and are sensitive to who is close to us.

- When out for a meal, we will "go Dutch," i.e., each pay for her own. This is to prevent that awful little squabble women in a restaurant always have over the check and to let us each eat, drink, and pay for whatever we choose without concern for the other's wallet.

- Barbara will make the arrangements for any joint travel because she is good at it and likes to do it, as I absolutely do not.

- Each of us will take the lead in social occasions that involve our own friends and family and will do the driving to get places with them.

- But Barbara will do any driving after dark because I cannot see well enough.

- When we start walking arm in arm together, I will be the one to adapt my step to hers.

- Only rarely, and mostly when we have other guests as well, will we share meals with one another. This way we will avoid much trivial conversation about diets, foods, shopping, recipes, and so forth.

- We will not use the word "lesbian" about ourselves, and we will avoid the expression "coming out" because that would confuse others about what our experience has been. We have not been "in the closet." We are women who, in our seventh decade, happen to have fallen for each other.

- We will not use crude words when referring to our sexual experiences.

We cannot possibly reveal everything to one another, nor should we, but we have promised we will answer any question honestly. I think this also makes us considerate about what questions we will ask. For example, I have made it a rule for myself that I will not ask about the details of Barb's life with Ken and especially not about their sex life.

We tried to set up a standard of avoiding too many rituals and routine so that we won't end up in some boring ruts of behavior. For example, Barb will not always run to her back window for a last goodnight when I have just left her bed and house. And I will not always gaze after her when she has left mine.

Even so, it turns out that at least one or two routines have become beloved and important. One is that I will stop by Barbara's place for ten minutes just before 9 a.m. every day but Saturday for a kiss and a hug and a quick review of each one's plans for the day ahead. On Saturday, we make it 10 a.m., and most of the time she comes to me. Within a few weeks, doing without this crucial connection early in every day felt painful.

We are still discussing, a year into it, whether to make a ritual of lying together two or three predictable evenings each week or to keep it more spontaneous. Either way, we are allowing for those afternoons when we cannot stay away from one another.

We have an agreement that we will not say, "I love you," every time we part company or hang up the phone lest that phrase become a near-meaningless habit. We try not to respond with, "I love you, too," when the other says it first because that can become manipulative on the one side and false on the other. When we do say, "I love you," it is deeply felt and expresses real-time feeling. Sometimes we try to find more specific words for showing appreciation and affection. Kisses, embraces, and eye-to-eye gazes are often better than words.

Our religious perspectives are quite different, even though we attend the same worship group together most Sundays. Barbara is a pretty solid atheist, whereas I call myself a religious post-theist. (I was a believer and a mystic for decades but lost my faith in a personal God in my fifties.) Our rule of thumb is to leave this topic alone on the whole.

We sit together in worship, in movies and concerts, and sometimes at big community meetings. But when one of us is in a leadership role at a committee meeting or event, the other stays pretty far back so as not to impede that role. Also to admire from afar! We always debrief it afterward.

We adhere to that popular saying, "Don't sweat the small stuff!" Fortunately, it comes naturally to both of us to let the little glitches go by, learning about one another in the process. We also know that when any small stuff begins to develop into a problematic pattern, we need to call for a problem-solving session.

However, another common teaching is tricky for us. "If you have nothing nice to say, don't say anything." Barb admits that because of this idea, she might go months before she shares a simple concern. We agree that the trick is to speak up forthrightly in a problem-solving tone. No saying "you always" or "just like your mother." (Perhaps it is a fortunate thing that Barbara and I are much too old to have known one another's mother!)

My father had a rule we rejected without much discussion. He used to say, "Don't let the sun set on your rage." (Is that from the Bible somewhere?) It meant my childhood was often plagued by the arguing voices of my parents far into the night. Barb and I agree that, instead, we will name the problem and set a date for dealing with it, then calm down, count to ten, sleep on it, and take it up later.

Our most important rule is that we won't share an apartment, as I have explained earlier. Some days I wonder if we might be shortchanging our "marriage" by this decision. But we reaffirm it constantly.

For one thing, there are no large apartments available in this senior community now, and 525 square feet is just too small for two large people. Also, we know that often in a shared household, one partner dominates in terms of how the space is decorated and used, what treasured possessions are kept, how the couple interacts with friends. After decades of independence in such matters and after downsizing radically to move to this retirement community in the first place, neither of us is inclined to give up more.

We are in and out of one another's apartments often and often for hours at a time. But spending the full night, as we would have to do if we shared an apartment, is not much of a temptation. Nights for people our age are often fraught with discomforts—insomnia, leg cramps, hot flashes, snoring or sleep apnea, flatulence, breathing problems, acid reflux, C-pap machines. It is easier to deal with any of these if we are not also disturbing a beloved partner. We are not afraid to be alone at night and can easily get help if we need it.

So far, we are also not sharing meals very often. We have different eating schedules, diets, preferences, and habits. For example, I've enjoyed reading at my solo table for some forty years now, and it would be hard to give that up. Ordinary quotidian conversation is not as interesting as the material in the books I read. And my meals are often haphazard, made up of random leftovers or eggs and toast. Who would want to give up that freedom?

We know that much of the trivial conversation of ordinary couples is around food—how and where it is bought, prepared, served, eaten, cleaned up, and stored. We can work together on all that occasionally, especially when we are entertaining friends (at my house if a table for four is large enough, at hers for five or more). But we are not inclined to do it two or three times a day. We prefer to share wine and cheese at the end of the day, with or without other friends.

One gets the impression that many younger couples are living this way nowadays. If children are not involved in a partnered relationship, a shared home and garden may not be called for. And everywhere, single family homes are becoming prohibitively expensive.

But perhaps in a high-rise city apartment building, getting from one apartment to the other might be less comfortable than it is here; there would be elevators and long hallways. The kind of senior community in which we live is the perfect setting. Here, the paths we take between our apartments are lined with gardens, trees, lawns, and casual friends, and even at night are well lit and safe. So walking between apartments is part of the pleasure we share.

4. The search for poetry

All through our first six months, we searched for poetry that would express the intense feelings we were experiencing. Barbara found the best ones, starting with one by **Adrienne Rich** that spoke to us strongly.

> Sleeping, turning in turn like planets
> rotating in their midnight meadow:
> a touch is enough to let us know
> we're not alone in the universe, even in sleep:
>
> . . .
>
> I've wakened to your muttered words
> spoken light-or dark-years away
> as if my own voice had spoken.

(From "XII" in *Twenty-One Love Poems*, 1976.)

In books and online, we sought out poems about love and romance between two women or for any love poems that could apply to us. A big volume of classic man-woman love poetry was almost completely useless. It was dismaying to find so many poems there that were about heartbreak, rejection, separation, or death.

Poets known to be lesbian often did not write about lesbian experience. Perhaps until recently it has not been thought safe. But Barbara found a few more by **Adrienne Rich**, and some by other women.

From "Floating Poem, Unnumbered" in *The Dream of a Common Language: Poems 1974–1977*, 1978.

> Whatever happens with us, your body
> will haunt mine—tender, delicate
> your lovemaking, like the half-curled frond
> of the fiddlehead fern in forests
> ...
> the innocence and wisdom of the place
> my tongue has found there—

From Poem II from "Twenty-One Love Poems" in *The Dream of a Common Language: Poems 1974–1977*, 1978.

> You've kissed my hair
> to wake me. *I dreamed you were a poem,*
> I say, *a poem I wanted to show someone…*
> and I laugh and fall dreaming again
> of the desire to show you to everyone I love,

From Poem III from "Twenty-One Love Poems" in
*The Dream of a Common Language: Poems 1974–
1977*, 1978.

> Since we're not young, weeks have to do time
> for years of missing each other. Yet only this odd
>   warp
> in time tells me we're not young.
>
> . . .
>
> At twenty, yes, we thought we'd live forever.
> At forty-five, I want to know even our limits.
> I touch you knowing we weren't born tomorrow,
> and somehow, each of us will help the other live,
> and somewhere, each of us must help the other die.

From "Love at Fifty" by **Marcia Woodruff** in *When I
Am an Old Woman I Shall Wear Purple*, 2007.

> We come together shy as virgins
> with neither beauty nor innocence
> to cover our nakedness, only
> these bodies which have served us well
> to offer each other.
>
> . . .
>
> "We are real," you say, and so we are,
> standing here in our simple flesh
> whereon our complicated histories are written,
> our bodies turning into gifts
> at the touch of our hands.

From "September afternoon at four o'clock" by
Marge Piercy in The Moon Is Always Female, 1980.

Full in the hand, heavy
with ripeness, perfume spreading
its fan: moments now resemble
sweet russet pears glowing
on the bough, peaches warm
from the afternoon sun, amber
and juicy, flesh that can
make you drunk.

. . .

Take,
eat, we are each other's
perfection, the wine of our
mouths is sweet and heavy.

The fruit is ripe for the taking
and we take. There is
no other wisdom.

Christina Rosetti (1830–1894) calls up a classic question we recognized:

> I loved you first, but afterwards your love,
> Outsoaring mine, sang such a loftier song
> As drowned the friendly cooings of my dove.
>
> Which owes the other most? My love was long,
> And yours one moment seemed to wax more strong;
> I loved and guessed at you, you construed me
> And loved me for what might or might not be —
> Nay, weights and measures do us both a wrong.
>
> For verily, love knows not 'mine' or 'thine;'
> With separate 'I' and "Thou' free love has done,
> For one is both, and both are one in love:
> Rich love knows nought of 'thine that is not mine;'
> Both have the strength and both the length thereof,
> Both of us, of the love that makes us one.

A few men seemed to express ideas and feelings we recognized.

First **Robert Graves:**

From "The Thieves."

> After, when they disentwine
> You from me and yours from mine,
> Neither can be certain who
> Was what I whose mine was you.

Then several from **E. E. Cummings** with his imaginative punctuation:

From *XAIPE*, 1950.

> the great advantage of being alive
> (instead of undying)is not so much
> that mind no more can disprove than prove
> what heart may feel and soul may touch
> —the great(my darling)happens to be
> that love are in we,that love are in we
>
> and here is a secret they never will share
> for whom create is less than have
> or one times one than when times where—
> that we are in love,that we are in love:
> with us they've nothing times nothing to do
> (for love are in we am in i are in you)

this world(as timorous itsters all
to call their cowardice quite agree)
shall never discover our touch and feel
—for love are in we are in love are in we;
for you are and i am and we are(above
and under all possible worlds)in love

a billion brains may coax undeath
from fancied fact and spaceful time—
no heart can leap, no soul can breathe
but by the sizeless truth of a dream
whose sleep is the sky and the earth and the sea,
for love are in you am in I are in we

Barbara quotes from this one constantly:

From 95 Poems, 1958.

i carry your heart with me(carry it in
my heart)am never without it(anywhere
i go you go, my dear;and whatever is done
by only me is your doing, my darling
                                    i fear
no fate(for you are my fate, my sweet)i want
no world(for beautiful you are my world,my true)
and it's you are whatever a moon has always meant
and whatever a sun will always sing is you

here is the deepest secret nobody knows
here is the root of the root and the bud of the bud
and the sky of the sky of a tree called life;which grows
higher than soul can hope or mind can hide)
and this is the wonder that's keeping the stars apart

i carry your heart(carry it in my heart)

My long-ago husband romanced me with this **Cummings** classic, but it works now, too:

From &[AND], 1925.

i like my body when it is with your
body. It is so quite new a thing.
Muscles better and nerves more.
i like your body like what it does,
i like its hows like to feel the spine
of your body and its bones,and the trembling
-firm-smoothness and which i will
again and again and again
kiss, i like kissing this and that of you,
i like,slowly stroking the, shocking fuzz
of your electric fur,and what-is-it comes
over parting flesh....And eyes big love-crumbs,

and possibly like the thrill
of under me you quite so new

And I could send this marvelous poem to Barbara now:

From "VII" in *is* 5, 1926.

since feeling is first
who pays any attention
to the syntax of things
will never wholly kiss you;

wholly to be a fool
while Spring is in the world

my blood approves,
and kisses are a better fate
than wisdom
lady i swear by all flowers.Don't cry
—the best gesture of my brain is less than
your eyelids' flutter which says

we are for each other:then
laugh,leaning back in my arms
for life's not a paragraph

And death I think is no parenthesis

Barbara sent me a **Rumi** poem, saying, "This definitely describes how I often feel," and I was just as drunk in those early days:

From "Intoxicated by Love."

> Because of your love
> I have lost my sobriety
> I am intoxicated
> by the madness of love
>
> In this fog
> I have become a stranger to myself
> I'm so drunk
> I've lost the way to my house
>
> In the garden
> I see only your face
> from trees and blossoms
> I inhale only your fragrance
>
> Drunk with the ecstasy of love
> I can no longer tell the difference
> between drunkard and drink
> Between Lover and Beloved.

Barbara sent me many cards in the early days with wonderful messages. In one, she wrote out by hand a **Rumi** poem:

> Know that my beloved is hidden from everyone.
> Know that she is beyond the belief of all beliefs.
> Know that in my heart she is as clear as the moon.
> Know that she is the life in my body and in my soul.

5. Living alone together

Most couples as thoroughly committed as we are, legally married or not, live together, sharing home and bed. Therefore, some days I wonder if we might be short-changing our "marriage" by persisting in living separately, albeit only a short distance apart. Are we more engaged than married? No, because engagement implies the plan to marry. But we are more than just "an item." We are life partners.

We have tried to resist getting too predictable in our daily habits as a couple but have settled into a flexible routine, nonetheless. We can always change it as needed.

In between our times together, morning and evening, we are often present at the same community gatherings or committee meetings, sitting together or across a room or table. In those contexts, being discreet and task oriented, we connect with one another almost no differently from anyone else. Sometimes that is so disorienting that afterward, to reestablish our close personal connection, we fall into one bed or the other in the middle of the afternoon!

Any part of any body can be viewed and touched and loved from any angle and perspective. Soaking up the various views of Barbara's body, I began to want to draw and paint what I saw. That led to an intense phase of study and effort to draw female nudes, alone and together. There are fewer examples in the literature than one would have hoped for. The teacher of my painting class gave her blessing and let me work at home for a few weeks, since I didn't want to explain to classmates why I was obsessed with female nudes.

Though we are two women of the same accomplished age and substantial size, it is most interesting how different the specifics of our bodies are. So much to learn! In several respects, we respond differently. But our basic compatibility up and down the whole range of variables is a source of wonder and gratitude for us. Not least is our propensity to humor—to be flirtatious, mischievous, to laugh and giggle, in bed and out. When you are really happy, it is easy to be foolish and giddy.

We keep learning the ways in which our temperaments and preferences are different. I always avoid mingling in big crowds, whereas Barbara is more comfortable in such sociable environments. I spend more time with individual friends than she. Our post-Christian and post-theist religious views are similar, but I am more engaged in the Quaker community and likely to remain so. Barbara is more relaxed about spending money and carbon footprint than I am.

We hold in common many traits, however. We each keep a clean and tidy house—this is SO important. (I lived with a hoarder once.) We read, we write serious material, we share a similar vocabulary. We like big words. We have the same sense of humor—what is more basic to a long-term relationship? Oh, gosh, we both make lists all the time, *to-do* lists. And like Doris Lessing, we keep different notebooks for different topics—it is too funny.

Neither of us is prone to jealousy, a tremendously important fact. Our views about death and dying are similar, and we are committed to helping one another to avoid heroics and histrionics when the time comes. We agree not to let our conversation get bogged down in trivia—and we agree that trivia is tricky to define.

We share a sensitive level of tact and care, I think, that keeps us from making remarks that would not be helpful. We try to let little glitches and disagreements slide right by, and when we have nothing positive to say, we keep quiet. At the same time, we are deeply committed to honesty. And we are aware of the danger in withholding fears and antagonisms that need expression and resolution.

We spent much of the third and fourth months of our liaison in finding good ways to let our closest friends and family members know what was going on with us. Then we started bringing people here where we live into our confidence. It was always fascinating to watch how people reacted and to hear what they said. Of course, almost always, people hook back into whatever previous experience they have had with two women being together, and often they assume we are long-time repressed lesbians. Nobody here seems distressed by it, though one or two found it a novel idea. Many say they know women who got together in mid-life. Almost no one seems the least concerned with our age. Of course, no one knows in detail what youthful behavior we are engaging in! We are revealing only part of the surprising story. It's fun.

Weeks ahead of time, we began to plan to make a small but semi-formal Sunday morning announcement to members of our faith community about our mutual commitment and our identity as a couple. After such an announcement, we thought, maybe we would be more relaxed about walking together, touching a little when others are around, and entertaining as a couple. *Will I be able to call her "darling" out loud in public?* But we have always been eager not to make anyone uncomfortable. Remember the rule: no kissing in front of other people! The residents here are probably more liberal, both politically and personally, than some of the staff members, and we will be considerate of them as well.

In any case, when we are publicly visible here, we are often as task oriented as everyone else. We are both community leaders in different ways. It is a delight to watch one another at the head of a table or in the front of a room, fulfilling leadership functions. In clothes and glasses, we can both appear quite austere and even stern, with never a hint of the mischievousness and lasciviousness we share at home. On the other hand, we both are known for an unrestrained loud laugh when the time is right.

There is almost nothing about our decisions and behavior that would be any different for a newly in-love, straight couple. In fact, there have been such couples in this community several times, people well into their seventies and eighties: a new couple about every five years, we figure. Often as not, they too did not legally marry and kept separate apartments with easy visiting privileges. Cooking and eating together may have been handled differently, and sex surely plays out in different ways, depending on libido and capacity. But gender differences fade away to almost nothing. I mean, for us, after the first few weeks, there was rarely any thought about how this would be different with a man, even though men are all we've known our whole lives.

Telling people about being in love has a shadow side to it, as many of our confidants might yearn to have such a rare opportunity themselves. It is poignant to realize that your happy news makes a dear friend wistful or lonely. For me, it is very important to follow up with substantive indications that I will not abandon my prior friendships. Barbara does not require me to change the habits and nature that attracted her to me in the first place. We do not want to lose ourselves in one another.

Barbara talks about the "intersecting trajectories" that everywhere bring people together unexpectedly, and we are fully aware of how our paths could have failed by mere inches to intersect. It was not a simple matter of physically meeting. A lot of other variables had to line up right. To extend the metaphor, imagine a gate with a combination lock at the place where two paths meet. The tumblers in the lock need to line up in just the right way at just the right moment for you to gain entry. So it has been for us. Barbara wrote:

> Can it really be true
> that each of us,
> so self-sufficient and
> complete in ourselves,
> has made a place
> for the other
> in her life?

It was hard to believe, even though we knew that the strongest partnerships can be formed by two individuals who are each self-sufficient and complete in themselves.

- I have learned so many new things about myself and others as well.

- I've known myself to be increasingly androgynous over the last couple of decades. With Barbara, there seems to be elicited from me an additional masculine kind of gentleness, protectiveness, and desire that I have not known before. It gives me a new understanding of men.

- I suddenly see all big and big-breasted women in a new way—I know and appreciate more now what they are like under their clothes, how they look and feel. (Of course, I am no pipsqueak myself, either.)

- I better understand the passion some older women have for being with their grandchildren, especially the littlest ones, where physical contact is so constant.

- I understand more about lesbian sexuality, its attractions and challenges, although we have had no personal experience with lesbian history, culture, or lifestyle.

For a while, Barbara claimed she had almost never had a best friend and now could happily claim me as one such, without yet saying more, to one or two relatives and colleagues. I have always had a best friend and several next-to-best as well, perhaps because I have not had a husband these past forty years. It was to these friends that I first revealed our secret, getting blessings and hearing their concerns, one at a time. It seemed as though each one, playing her part in my history, had helped to pave my accidental path to Barbara.

6. Under a leading?

I am a member of the Religious Society of Friends, more commonly called Quakers, a historically Protestant group. Barbara hangs out with us, too. We Quakers, like everyone else, occasionally find ourselves on the verge of some life-changing undertaking or change of path. Sometimes these ideas seem to come from out of the blue.

- Maybe I should transfer to another college and marry this man.

- Maybe I should write a book about Quaker values.

Quakers have special expressions that may come into play: Perhaps I am *under a leading* to adopt a child. Is *the way opening* for me to leave my husband and finish raising four children alone? Maybe I am *called* to join a peace team in Iraq. Historically, Quakers perceive God or a divine guide as doing the leading.

- Could it be that now I am being led to take up with another woman?

Often a person's first reaction to a leading is, "Oh, no, not me!" The path opening up may seem impossible, foolhardy, or perhaps dangerously motivated by desperate need or ego and arrogance. There is a hazard in too easily using the idea that "God is calling me" to justify a self-serving notion or a plan that will be hurtful to others. To protect the seeker against such a misstep, Quakers have long relied upon a process of *seeking clearness* in order to *test the leading*. In traditional terms, the challenge is to explore whether the leading is truly *Spirit-led*.

Often a formal *clearness committee* is established to meet several times with the seeker and help her explore all aspects of the *leading* before she makes a commitment to the new path or project. In other situations, conversations with a series of friends serves this purpose equally well. Issues explored can include motivation, logistics, finances, capacity to follow through, and consequences for others.

If, after these conversations, both mind and heart of the seeker are clear and easy about the decision to go ahead, then she may conclude that *the leading is Spirit-led*, and the *way is open*. She has *reached clearness* and can *proceed under divine guidance*. Challenges will emerge along the way, but they will be met in good faith and with the help and support of friends.

What happens to ideas about divine leadings and clearness when a person does not believe in a personal

God who guides and guards her through major decisions and undertakings? The sense of calling can still arise, slowly or suddenly. What is happening, then, if it isn't God at work?

It was years ago, when struggling with this question, that I first encountered the metaphorical concept of a combination lock I mentioned earlier. As the dial moves, the internal tumblers are opened one at a time until suddenly the final tumbler is moved back, the piston falls through, and the lock is released. *The way opens*, as Quakers would say. Sometimes the seeker had no awareness of the process or even of a door that had been locked.

Slowly it began to seem to me that *I* was *under a leading* to be the committed partner of Barbara Benham Tye. Certainly, my first reaction when the possibility emerged was the classic, "Oh, no, not me!" Never before in my life was I aware of any inclination toward such an attraction or commitment. I had no idea that the door was there and that all but the last tumbler was open that day in March when I first suddenly saw what Barbara could be to me. Certainly, since then, I have been through a long and intense *clearness process* with a series of trusted friends who have tested my capacity to pursue this *opening*.

The click-back of the tumblers was the necessary prerequisite that allowed me to engage with another woman at this late stage of my life. When Barbara and I fell together on that momentous day in March, I already knew at a semi-conscious level about our compatibility. Other tumblers were already open:

- We each had enough maturity, experience, and self-confidence to stand as an equal partner side by side in a balanced relationship where neither one was too needy or dependent upon the other.

- We were both free of excessive obligations to others.

- We were both financially independent in a modest sort of way.

- Our political and personal values were fully complementary.

- Especially important at our age, our attitudes toward dying and death were the same

Then suddenly, the last tumbler clicked back. We suddenly discovered that there was a strong erotic spark between us. *The way opened* when I realized, all unexpected, that I could hold this woman in my arms and in my heart unreservedly. Pow! Just like that!

Only after that realization did I start on the *clearness process* and assure myself that the necessary underlying conditions for commitment were in place.

First there was our agreement not to marry legally or to share a home. Then we found that we both had adequate health, stamina, and libido to share full-fledged in the sexual aspects of this partnership. We had enough experience living alone to be confident we would be able to let sexuality go when the time came. We felt we could stand by one another through the end-of-life challenges. We are fortunate to live in a time of history, a state of the nation, and an immediate community that support our decision. All our close family and friends are both encouraging and welcoming.

The major turning points in my life have all involved pursuit of leadings in this way, and I recognized this as just one more. Barbara doesn't think in these terms, really, but the process for her has been similar. Reaching a state of *clearness* and sufficient confidence to make personal and public commitments took us many weeks—about three months—before we "pledged our troth" to one another. It was another two months or so before we stood up in a gathering of our faith community to declare ourselves a couple.

Of course, we know there will be further questions and challenges. We are committed to deal with them together, with whatever human and divine guidance might be available. "We'll get by with a little help from our friends," as the song says.

Now there is another question on my mind: Am I *under a leading* to create a written record of our experiences for a public audience, to write this book?

7. Established

It is July. Barbara and I are well into what you might call the second trimester of this new relationship. We are not sending more than one love letter per day. We are not singing all the old love songs, amazed at how they constantly pop up from deep memory. Our e-mail messages don't have quite so many emoticons across the bottom. We have passed several milestones.

- We have declared our lifetime commitment to one another.

- We are clear that we have not become lesbians.

- We have told all our close family and friends our news.

- We have stopped being secretive among our neighbors.

- We have learned a lot about our bodies.

- We have grappled with changes in self-image and proven our constancy with other friends and family.

Commitment

Commitment has involved living through early shock and surprise, careful definition of what we are doing here, and some ceremonial confirmation.

How surprising it was to find that almost immediately upon falling into one another's arms, we were eager to promise and pledge our primary love and care to one another until the end of our days. I never made such promises, early or late, to the men I knew after my husband, not even to my lover of twelve years. So why in this case bind ourselves so quickly?

Perhaps it is because of our age and the fact that the timeline 'til death us do part is relatively short, though we are both in basically good health so far. Perhaps it is because we live in an intense cooperative community where casual romance could make people uneasy. Perhaps it is because, having known one another as neighbors for a year, we already knew how well-matched we were, how compatible on many counts. I have recognized Barbara as that independent-thinking partner I was hoping for.

It was still very scary at first. But we clarified rapidly that commitment for us does not mean legal marriage (which would bind our finances together); or cohabitation in the same household (which would complicate daily life a lot); or giving up occupations and involvements important to either of us; or promising to be the constant solo bedside caregiver should the necessity arise. It does not require disrupting the needs and expectations of any dependents. In fact, our elderly situation in a liberal and open-minded senior community is the perfect supportive environment in which to bring such a new relationship to life.

There are also logistical reasons for not having a wedding or ceremony of commitment.

- We don't want to mingle our money and possessions, neither needing more than she currently has and each having family who stand to inherit.

- Being so long experienced, we don't need others to test our intention and ability to commit, or to take our relationship "under their care," as the Quaker community would offer to do.

- Being atheist (Barb) and post-theist (me), we are not in need of a religious element to our commitment.

- We do not want to involve others in a lot of planning, expense, carbon footprint for travel to a wedding event, or for gifts that we don't need.

So, over the course of many weeks, we committed ourselves to one another in various other ways. Barbara took off her wedding ring and bought that double bed. And then, on June 6, she arranged a little ceremony on a special hilltop during which she introduced me to her departed husband, thanking him for all he had meant to her, and remembering how he had encouraged her to find a new love. Sitting knee to knee and holding both hands, she and I promised ourselves to one another 'til the end of our time.

Not lesbian

We two have both lived intimately and happily with men most of our adult lives. We are clear that, while "lesbian" has commonly been the adjective used for sexual congress involving two women and in that sense applies to some of our behavior together, we have not suddenly become gay, and neither one of us has been yearning for a female lover all these years.

The first person I told about this astonishing thing that was happening to us was a friend of some forty years who is gay. The first thing she said to me was, "This doesn't make you a lesbian, you know." Of course, she was right. We do not have the history, social scars, acculturation, or expectations of the lesbian community, and we would disrespect and devalue our sisters in that group if we thought we could belong with them simply by having lain together.

Pansexuality and androgyny are more useful concepts for us to explore after six decades of being actively involved with men. As our own young relatives (and the *New York Times*) point out, pansexual generally means, "Someone who is attracted to a person's qualities regardless of their gender identity" (NYT, Sunday June 24, 2018). A niece of mine in her early thirties, and a granddaughter barely twenty-one, told us, when each in turn heard our news, that the time has passed when people should define themselves in an artificially binary fashion as straight or gay. We all have multiple capacities and live along a continuum of sexual orientation and attraction, they insisted. I like that so much. Pansexuality seems congruent with the concept of androgyny I have been pursuing for years.

Being educated, advantaged, and liberated white women who in our adult years have always had gay and lesbian friends, we both had opportunities for different kinds of close relationships with women but always steered away from romantic ones. Now some friends think we are brave to get involved with one another. However, it is only in not resisting the overwhelming impulse to fall in love that we are brave. We did not plan, need, want, or choose this romance to happen. We were, both of us, astonished and considerably disturbed. But despite the confusion and moments of terror, we each chose not to push back, not to walk away. It is surely because of all the positive things we had learned from and about gay people all our adult years that we were able to accept what was happening to us, able to have the courage to go forward with it and with each other.

Telling others

Once we began to get used to each other, we spent much time and effort on figuring out how to tell people what was happening to us. We shared the news by handwritten note, e-mail, phone, or in person. Almost everyone has been surprised. Absolutely everyone has responded in a supportive way. (We assume, though, that a few were not comfortable, just polite.) Most people have not known quite what to say or ask, and many, assuming we are "coming out" as lesbians, have diverted the conversation pretty fast to stories of their own: Oh, yes, my aunt—etc.

We began to expect that more questions, concerns, and opinions would emerge in the second and third round of conversations with people. And so it has been. We knew we could wait until a little later, partly with this book, to correct the assumption that we were basically lesbians who had finally found one another.

One sister worried immediately that at our age, making a lifetime commitment put each of us at risk of being the main support and advocate for a dying partner soon. She is right; we thought of it from the first day. In an important way, that recognized hazard has deepened and enriched the wild enchanted discovery stage of this romance from the beginning. We have seen this connection as a big deal from day one. This was never a casual dalliance.

More people than I expected seem to be dealing for the first time with the concept of deep connection and physical love between two women. We thought that in California in 2018, no one would be taken aback, but it seems to be a new or disturbing concept to one or two of our generation. On the other hand, two or three friends are immediately grasping the late-life love option for themselves from the example we are setting. *Do we have a role in encouraging that?*

I thought our children, though modern and metro-savvy, might stumble a bit over the idea of an old grandmother being in a romance. Twenty-year-olds, sure, but old ladies? But our children seem OK with it.

My daughter groaned originally at the idea that it was a woman I had fallen for. She had always wanted some white knight to come along and sweep me away. But very quickly, even during that first phone conversation, she changed her tone and said the news had made her day. She said this development "rounds you out as a person, Mom." I guess that in her chaotic life until recently, she has seen me as a stalwart rock and a source of guidance and support but not as an ordinary, vulnerable woman!

Of course, we each now have an on-site advocate and friend to stand by us when the going gets rough. This must be something of a relief to our relatives, all of them at least eighty miles away, though they have not said so. They probably do not want to picture in any detail the fact that we are body-to-body lovers—bosom buddies, you could accurately call it. So be it.

We have gone to visit family and close friends in their homes all over Northern California and have had a series of visitors here. Each of us took the lead with our own close people. I took Barbara on a marathon tour of my three California children one weekend. She won over my daughter by pressing up close to her over the kitchen sink and whispering, "I was really nervous about us meeting; weren't you?"

We have begun to share the joys and cares of one another's families and to sort out how much we want to be involved. After some hesitation, I agreed to attend the upcoming wedding of a niece of Barbara; I couldn't bear her going there alone as a widow.

Neighbors in our resident community

Telling our neighbors about us was a bit of a hurdle to overcome even in this tolerant community. When we felt almost ready, we went to a neighboring lesbian widow for her advice and followed it: choose six to ten special friends in the community and tell them individually; then let the word seep out spontaneously.

As the news spread, some folks would come right up to us and say hurrah, but others were more shy or discreet about what they knew or guessed. After a while, it became hard, wondering who had gotten the news and who had not. We began to plan to bring everyone into our confidence with some kind of public announcement.

The fact that there had been a new romance every four to five years within this community of eighty to ninety elders encouraged us, even though always before it has involved a man and a woman. After all, our age is as much an astonishment as our mutual gender.

Our bodies

We count our blessings in the bodies we have, not yet too badly ravaged by age. We have our own teeth, can hear and track OK, laugh over the ritual of removing our glasses to embrace and kiss. Neither has lost a breast or a leg. Neither has any terminal disease so far.

However, it is also true that neither of us conforms to any conventional form of feminine beauty, although Barbara has a beautiful face when she smiles. We are old, wrinkled, overweight, arthritic, stiff, and sometimes lame. Barbara's knees are collapsing, so she walks in a knock-kneed way. (I adore that funny, characteristic gait of hers.) We both suffer from intermittent joint pain, leg cramps, and acid reflux. I've got low-grade asthma and often cough. These ailments become a source of hilarity between us as often as not.

We both hate to look in the mirror, but we know how to look at each other. We look at (I mean gaze in delight at) those parts of the other's body that enchant us, and never mind the rest. We stroke and caress more parts than we look at: feeling is as important a part of lovemaking as seeing at any age.

In many ways, we revel in the fact that, both being women, we recognize and know what to do with one another's bodies. But there are also many ways in which our bodies are different. So much to discover! Caressing Barbara's breasts excites me more than it does her. We never dreamed of touching the spaces and places between another woman's legs. The configurations there of bone and flesh are very different in important ways. *Are all women so different?* My well-experienced male lover of many years never hinted at such a thing. *How could I not have learned anything about this in all these decades?*

Our bodies respond in quite different ways to all the kissing and stroking we share. Orgasm has a different and broader meaning now. Satisfaction is multi-faceted and complete. We are still learning slowly what's good to do for one another. The certainty that our high level of libido will eventually decline intensifies our sense of good luck and joy in what we are sharing now.

Changing self-image

It seems that the impulse to move closer than mere friendship came slowly over time to Barbara. For me, it was virtually an overnight slam that really knocked me for a loop at first. Both of us had very satisfactory lives and no interest in adding anything romantic or extra. We both thought falling in love was a question of neediness, and we were not feeling needy.

Moreover, we felt for sure that we were too old and too straight to be falling for one another. I myself was surely far too independent, rational, and in control of my life to be overcome in this way. Shock! Confusion! *Who am I? What's going on? What will happen next? What will people say? How much will this disrupt my good life?*

But with what was happening when we lay down together, there was no turning back. Moreover, as we talked indefatigably about everything, we learned how compatible we are in terms of strengths, values, goals, and expectations for this relationship. We are very well matched in terms of intelligence, education, public activism, politics, commitment to our residential community, stamina, libido, and good humor. We are both writers and often talk together as colleagues about our writing projects.

On the other hand, we affirm the differences in our interests and commitments. Each wants to keep on doing most of what she did before, keep on being the same person that attracted the other in the first place. We don't want to lose ourselves in sameness and trivia. We don't want to do everything together.

As time has passed and we have been able to promise and demonstrate that we will keep up our previous friendships and commitments, others and we ourselves are increasingly confident that this is a sustainable relationship.

8. Our own early poems

We were disappointed not to find more poems like the first Adrienne Rich pieces we had come across, explicit glowing celebration of the most sensuous aspects of women's mutual experience. So, being a poet myself, I tried my hand at writing in this genre.

Revolution

Revolution used to involve
banners and barriers,
bloodshed and anger,
hurt and harassment,
masses of people.

Then just you by yourself
revolutionized my life
with one unexpected kiss
and a hand upon my breast.

Another woman's hand upon my breast!
Her lips right here, kissing mine!
My world revolved, evolved,
in total astonishment.

Crescent curve

In the late last light,
clothes slowly, lightly taken off
and kiss-caressing, gently
moving toward the bed,
I watch before we're
even lying down
to see the crescent curve
of shadow
at your rounded breast.

I always wondered: lips to nipple,
tongue and mouth upon a breast:
how would it feel? I know now,
love, and want again the bliss-caress,
the deepest kiss, and then my hand
far down there, darling,
yes and yes.

Lovestruck

Here I am, the all of me,
the who I was before, and now
the who I am because of how
you call me up and bring me out.
You bring me to the new of me
that never was in all my time,
that never was 'til now.

Your face, your mouth, your hands across
and fingers deep within myself,
your dazzling, darling, dear-heart eyes—
I'm new with you, entwined, engulfed,
enlarged, entangled. Hold, oh hold
me more and then again, so near,
my very darling dear.

Pledge

Drink to me only with thine eyes,
and I will pledge with mine.

Pledged and promised, sinking deep
into your gaze, gathering under,
into, and across all our lovely limbs,
agang and against long legs entwined,
thigh smoothing belly,
knee nuzzling nipple,
kisses on your face,
hands everywhere,
winding and binding us
to one another like bands of grace:
this is how we are together.

Disappearing

We went for the full tamasha,*
climbing in turns, reaching and peaking,
then slowly sank and settled
into a dark-surrounded silence,
wrapped and enraptured together.

I couldn't see your eye
an inch from mine
but felt its intense gaze.
Rapt and awed, I
heard in your steady breath
the essential rhythm of
life itself, sucking us under
until we began to disappear.

*Urdu for celebration

Embrace

Knowing your body means
discerning where to look and
what to feel,
how to kiss and
what to stroke.

I admire your beauties—
and absolutely adore
your lesser attributes,
embracing all your parts
with my legs as much as
with my arms
and with my heart.

All the ways of you

I love all the ways of you:
of course the you who
languishes full-breasted in my arms,
but also you who walks away
with that dear knock-kneed gait;
you as hostess attending all the little needs;
you as leader of the gathered people
(and there I watch the spotlight
fall upon your breast).

Rose wet cave*

The rose-wet cave seems
sometimes lush as green,
pulsing and pushing,
sucking like a sweet-tongued mouth.
My body trembles in response,
clasping and gasping.

The second time, that velvet glade
opens into wide lacey swathes
of swimming green,
a garden pool that sucks me down,
deepening into such delight, it's
hard to breathe, believe, or leave.

*Thanks to Adrienne Rich

Becoming divine

The body holds me wide-alive,
though the soul belongs
to somewhere else at last,
and only death
will close that gap.

Meanwhile, reaching deep
into the heart dark valley
of my darling seems entirely enough.
I gasp and grasp her
like the dying person I am,
my loins and longing
willing to make a newness,
a new life.

Nature is saying: take and make
from these ravishing
kisses and caresses
something new.
Lose and find yourself in
her dark places and embraces.
Oh, darling,
hold and hide my face;
extinguish me in you.
This kind of death is called ecstasy
when I become you, become we,
become something divine.

Far love

Oh, my dear darling,
let me hold and enfold,
embrace and entwine you
in the fine fierce fantasy of
belief that I and you,
oh, you too, darling,
are not alone.

Alone (with God or not)
is all how all we are.
We strive so hard to disbelieve it;
we love each other so
fervently well to make it not so.

But in the depths and
in the end, the whole
fervor and poignancy of
our reaching love is
to deny the reality of:
you alone and
me over here on another side,
oh, darling, my dear, my far love.

Dread and hope

Dread swells up,
then leans over and rests
on the comfy side of hope:
that the dire things that
could happen
will not.

Repeat: dire things
could happen
but will not,
leaving love good time
to flourish and to grow.

I am so wordy! It was Barbara who created a perfect two-stanza haiku—

> Your hungry eyes, your
> urgent kiss—my melting heart
> —unexpected bliss.
>
> Your laughing eyes, your
> feathery touch: happiness
> beyond words—too much.

—and a whole flock of tiny poems.

> The nipple of your right breast rises
> to greet my slowly circling fingertips.
>
> . . . .
>
> Our legs curl around each other,
> drawing us into one body.
>
> . . . .
>
> You touch me there,
> and I arch into joy.
>   Please—
>   please,
>   don't stop.

. . . .

Standing tall, these two
could be mistaken for
two sturdy oak trees.

. . . .

Which is the lover, which the loved?
The question is absurd; each is both.

. . . .

I'm not too old at all, she said,
and flung herself across the bed.

. . . .

Words of advice

Be delirious
—not serious.

Smile all the while.

Wiggle a little;
giggle a lot.

. . . .

There is an old woman whose blouse'll
come off at the slightest arousal.
With nothing else on, she'll
invite you to touch, feel
the start of an evening's carousal.

9. Androgyny

Ages and Stages

Barbara and I soon found that we would constantly have to push for a clearer definition of lesbianism. Women especially, upon hearing that we were together, would immediately start talking as though we were lesbians. They would assume that our romance was the resolution of a long-time discomfort in our lives, that we had each been on the lookout for a female partner for decades, or that we had at long last found our "true nature."

Wrong. It was my true nature, and a very enthusiastic one at that when, at age nineteen, I married a man who could make love to me like heck and could also make me a mother. At that stage of life, nothing was more important to me.

It was still my true nature two decades later when, after the marriage had ended and while living as a professional woman on my own, I dallied with a number of guys, then established a liaison with one fabulous lover. I would never have married him, not because he was an African immigrant, but because our obligations, temperaments, and values were too enormously different. We met only once every two weeks or so—for twelve years. He had other women, too. I didn't mind; he was too good a lover not to share. I liked our relationship just the way it was. Although I had been taught that such an uncommitted liaison was wrong, it was right for me at that stage.

We finally parted company, my long-time lover and I, because of age and the hazards of AIDS. After that, it was yet again another aspect of the true me when, in my mid-fifties, I took a vow of celibacy with the members of my women's group as witnesses. I vowed not to seek or make myself available to another man again. I experienced an exhilarating freedom to love the world at large and people in general, instead of having to focus the weight of my emotional energy on one limited individual. My children lived elsewhere by then, so I lived alone and exultant in that open-hearted condition for twenty-three years, a marvelous stage of life I could have pursued until my dying day.

But then Barbara Benham Tye showed up. There is nothing the least bit false or fabricated in my passion for her. This stage of my life is just as honest and grounded as any of the earlier ones. I am deeply grateful to have experienced these different ages and stages of life.

Pansexuality

Somewhere in the Hebrew Scriptures, according to one rich translation, when asked what he should be called, God refuses a name and says, "I am that I am." Perhaps another translation would have put it slightly differently: I am *what* I am.

Resonating to this passage over a couple of decades, I have come to believe that this is also the name for "that of God," for the divine essence, that is within me and all others. *I am what I am.* As long as I can make this statement without reservation, I know I am not playing myself false. I am living out my true nature.

The binary labels popular in the twentieth century are no longer useful in the twenty-first for understanding people. I love it that it is the young ones who are teaching me about this. A grandson insists: "Liliz, you are just who you are. You love who you love. No labels!"

A friend from high school talked long on the phone to me, testifying that she had especially enjoyed growing into her sixties, when both men and women around her were moving "beyond the impersonation acts" tying them to gender expectation.

"Instead of either-or, we encounter and-and," she declared fervently. A woman can find that she has female traits and perspectives AND male competencies, inclinations and sensibilities. I agreed with her. This is the mature androgyny that interests me so much.

Androgyny

My sense of it is that I am increasingly androgynous. I hope so: this is the condition I want to attain by the end of my life.

I do not mean, of course, that I dress in an ambiguous way so that people will not know for sure whether I am a woman or a man. I do not mean that I am a hermaphrodite or a "dyke." I do not mean that I am bisexual, from the start sexually attracted to both (all) genders.

I mean that for many years, I have had both the inclination and the opportunity to develop masculine aspects of my personality with the conscious goal of becoming an independent and integrated person, a whole *persona*. This process started long before I met Barbara.

Maybe I was able to take that vow of celibacy at age fifty-three because, by then, I had become a more balanced and whole person, an *androgyne*. Carl Jung would say that my *animus* was well developed. Both *anima* and *animus* have matured within my own psyche. Along with what are thought of as feminine traits, I have some of the capacities and sensibilities usually associated with men.

The researched facts about the midlife hormonal changes in men and women, which make them more and more alike as they age, have always fascinated me. We know that hormonal shifts after menopause (including "male menopause") have physiological effects on the personality as well as on the body, sometimes affording men easier access to their feelings and gentler inclinations, sometimes allowing women to become more confident and bold.

The Greeks claimed that we all look for a person of the opposite gender to complement our own character. In Ancient Chinese philosophy, the complementary forces of yin and yang are bound together to make a whole. Perhaps we have now learned that the whole can be held within a single person. Perhaps, sometimes, a woman of accomplished years and experience no longer feels that her femininity needs to be balanced by the intimate presence of a man in her life. Perhaps her androgynous, whole self will best be partnered by another independent, androgynous woman.

Masculine inclinations

For me, becoming more androgynous over these recent years has not meant becoming more controlling or "butch" but just experiencing my own capacity, confidence, and independence. In intimate relations with men, my feminine traits were evoked. With Barbara, the more masculine aspect of me is burgeoning. I can feel in turns like a randy boy or a dependent husband. I love being a little taller than she is; it sometimes makes me feel protective toward her, especially when we walk arm in arm. In clothes and in attitudes, I am often dark to her bright. I think about how to be a good lover in a way I never did when I was to be "taken" by a man.

I tried to express it in a poem:

> I want to come to you dark.
> I want to come to you strong,
> tall, and confident.
>
> I don't mean to mean
> that I want to come to you
> like a man,
> though I love the man in me.
>
> I am a tall, strong, and
> confident woman, darling,
> and you are the woman
> I want in my dark embrace
> tonight.

Jane Rule

One preparative experience for this development in my life was knowing Jane Rule, one of the most important leaders of lesbian awareness in our time. She is the author of several books including *Desert of the Heart* (1964), which later became a cutting-edge movie.

Before her development as a writer, Jane Rule taught English at the girls school I attended as a teenager and was my English teacher in sophomore and senior years. At that time, I did not know anything about the homoerotic aspects of sexual attraction. I did not have a crush on Jane Rule; it was blond, handsome, married Mr. Eddy that I and half my classmates were gaga about.

The thing that was attractive about Miss Rule, as we called her, was her intelligence, her self-control, and a certain subtle masculinity about her. I didn't fall for her; I wanted to be like her. Now, this summer, I have gotten deeply immersed in another of her books, curiously titled *This Is Not For You*, where these admired traits are portrayed in the character of Kate.

In the book, there is only one explicit love scene: a one-off event that involves the protagonist, Kate, with a woman other than her beloved, Esther. For Kate, her own performance as a lover is important; she is self-conscious and careful about it. Even for this one-night stand, she plans ahead. She has learned that, in bed, telling her partner what she is going to do next enhances the experience for both of them. I admire and aspire to such self-control—but because there is a manipulative aspect to it, perhaps it is just as well that I generally fail, literally collapsing into a wild and gasping embrace.

The androgynous impulse produces its poignant moments. Sometimes when I lean over my darling, I would so love to be able to merge with her as a man would. It makes the moment deeply poignant—and also unsustainable. There is no merit in thinking of what we cannot have.

I wonder how other women have experienced this kind of thing. But none of the literature we found said anything about the effects of an androgynous sensibility in women couples, not even June Singer's well-known book on androgyny. You'd think she might at least have differentiated bisexuality as a biological inclination from androgyny, which is a state of mind and sensibilities.

High libido

Maybe the operative factor through all the stages of my life has been a very lively libido. It is just something I was born with. I came by it honestly from my mother, poor frustrated woman. As a teen, I loved kissing and necking and dancing with the guys, nothing more than that was allowed. I married early in order to get access to the rest of it—and to get babies. After the babies, I stuck with my husband through years of misery because the sex was still so good. For some failing couples, it's the sex that drops away first. For us, sex was the last hurrah.

After the marriage, I stayed so long with a lover I couldn't marry because I loved what he did with me in bed. And even during my long years of celibacy, I was plenty orgasmic. It doesn't take two, of course.

And now with this woman who is the soul mate I have always wanted, sexuality still looms large. Am I just driven by sexual need? If so, it is not a point of pride, but at least it is not hurting anybody. I often think of sex as God's great comfort to us poor beleaguered humans.

Asexuality

High libido in me and Barbara may be one of the characteristics that differentiates us from some lesbians. In *Sexual Intimacy for Women*, Dr. Glenda Corwin describes a phenomenon many lesbians must know about but that we had not heard of before: the common issue of low libido among women in same-sex relationships. Only twenty percent of lesbian women are sexually active, Corwin tells us, citing numerous sources. "Active" is defined as engaging in sex twice a month. "Lesbian bed death" is a common expression that means sex dies out fast between women very often, according to many studies and common experience.

What Corwin does not discuss and what we wonder is whether many women who get with other women are not so much homosexual or bisexual but just plain not interested in sex at all. Thus, asexual. Presumably, it is easier to hide and manage this disinterest in a hypersexed society with another low-libido woman than in a conventional male-female marriage—although, surely, some men also have very low libido.

We are not all interested in sex all the time, as American culture often wants us to believe. According to much of advertising, TV, movies, even books, no one is supposed to be asexual in our society. But it is probable that lots of people have no real interest in sex from the time they are young. Some of us feel "unsexed" by surgeries and waning hormones, but others never felt the urge at all. Some of you reading these pages might be curious, perhaps slightly repelled. *Who cares about sexuality that much?* you'll be wondering. Maybe you do not, and I do. Does it matter?

10. Public commitment

We did it. We married, insofar as we will marry. It is not a conventional marriage but definitely a commitment.

Early on that morning, July 22, I went to Barbara to kiss her into the day and check in on our mutual plans and well-being. She put a necklace around my neck, a three-piece medallion of carved old jade: oh, it is gorgeous. She says she did not plan it ahead, it just came to hand the day before, and that I must not worry that I, who had tried for weeks to find the right token of love and commitment for her, had failed so far.

Two hours later, we stood up in front of our faith community, our Quaker worship group, during the announcement time, and told the Friends gathered there that we considered ourselves a couple.

So here's the picture: something like twenty-two people and a service dog have been sitting in silence in a double circle in the library, books all around, for an hour. Meeting closes with the clasping of your neighbor's hand and murmured greetings. Someone passes the microphone around so each can introduce him or herself. Then announcements: our cue.

Together we had carefully drafted and edited the two simple paragraphs and even kind of rehearsed them—and then as we stood there, my hand on Barb's shoulder so she could hold the mic in one hand and the paper in the other, we said what came to us at the moment. We testified to our commitment before that small group of our old friends seated there, perhaps half of whom already knew that we counted ourselves as a couple. Here's what we had planned to say and more or less did.

Barbara:

> It is with great joy that we rise together to testify that over the past five months, we have grown increasingly close. To our great surprise, we have come to consider ourselves as partners, as a couple. We have committed ourselves to one another for whatever time remains to us, "Til death us do part." Our families—siblings, in-laws, children, and grandchildren—are all supportive, as are far-flung friends.

Elizabeth:

> For many weeks we have been preparing to
> declare our commitment in this simple way
> to this circle of Friends—you, who are part
> of our faith community. Today, it feels right
> to speak.

> We do not feel led toward legal marriage or
> a formal ceremony of commitment. We will
> not give up our separate apartments. Before
> we knew each other, we were each deeply
> committed to this community, and we feel
> well supported here.

Then I added that we wanted their help in spreading the word amongst all our neighbors.

At the rise of meeting, people greeted and thanked and hugged and encouraged us. Oh, it was a relief to go public this way! No one urged us to have any kind of celebration, though we had thought they might.

One or two folks did ask us if we are going to have some sort of a honeymoon, and we are!

We were already planning to travel across the country by train in October, going first to Chicago on Amtrak's wonderful California Zephyr, and thence to Washington, DC. Barbara would make all the arrangements, blessings on her: she likes doing that sort of thing, which I do not. We planned to stop over one night in Chicago, where she had lived for years, and to visit the Art Institute there, a great treat.

The fact that this trip was basically to get me to DC to do a good-Samaritan stint for two weeks just fit within our view of how life should be lived. Barbara, too, traveling back home alone, would visit friends and finish up lingering business in a city or two that would keep her away from home while I was away so as to reduce our separation time.

On the Zephyr, we would have a sleeping compartment, a luxury I never indulged in before, a romantic experience that would surely round out my appreciation of Amtrak passenger services.

It was a funny thing to be looking forward to three days and nights cloistered together as an opportunity, finally, to ask Barbara a lot about her past. We had been so attentive those first five months to learning how to interact with one another and how to share our status as a couple with others that we had talked very little about our past experiences—but had committed ourselves to one another anyway.

I knew very little about Barb's professional life, about her travels, or her stints with Ken in Oslo, Dubai, and Djakarta. We hadn't talked much about her experiences with Ken's children. She'd have a chance to ask me anything she wanted about my work, my colleagues, my life in Pakistan, India, and San Francisco. Or perhaps it would emerge that all this ancient history, the detail of it, was of no importance to us. Perhaps knowing who we are now, no matter how we got here, is all we really want to know. Either way, we were eager for the experience.

Eventually, maybe ten days after our July 22 declaration, we became pretty sure that all who live in this community and pay any attention to others (there are some who do not) were aware of our new amorous status. During those days, we turned our attention to the staff, speaking individually to those closest to us and trusting to the affable grapevine thereafter. We encountered no negativity, hardly even any surprise.

Barbara was more nervous than I was in the days before our public testimony. For me, the scary part had been weeks before, on June 6, just the two of us together, when I promised myself to her on that hilltop. This public stuff was just a small follow-up ritual. But private and public commitment together didn't end my occasional moments of panic. *What have I done? Do I have any idea what I am doing? Who am I, even? For a few episodes of blissful sex, have I given away my future? Ach, where is she anyway?*

But then, back in her arms (we never enter a private room together without an immediate embrace), I'd forget my anxiety. Of course, it is a slow process to give up one's independence after some forty years of living on your own.

In the follow-up to our public announcement, we continued to be fascinated by the way people responded. They asked again about legal marriage, moving in together, what our families thought. Of course, no one asked a thing about how much time we spend together and how often, when and where we were lying together. American advertisements link everything to sexual attraction, but American people tend to be very secretive about sexual activity. Why is that? Is it that old Puritan ethic that erroneously thinks sexuality is somehow evil or unhealthy? I think of it as a divine blessing.

One or two friends asked us whether we had talked to our doctors. My experience had been confirmed by Robert Butler in his book about sexuality and aging: most doctors don't inquire about an older person's sex life even when doing a general physical exam or health review. Sexual matters only come up if the (shy) patient initiates.

Shy or not, I wanted to brag to my primary physician that I was having this happy new experience. I also needed to ask her if my long-standing, mostly inactive herpes would cause a problem. The conversation was short. About the first, she just said, "Great!" About the second: "When you have any overt symptoms, avoid oral sex."

Friends prodded us about getting legal access to one another's medical information, advance directives, and hospital rooms, should the time come. We are working on all that. Each of us already had identified a legal health advocate or DPA for end-of-life decisions. Whether to change those assignments and take on those roles for one another was a major topic of discussion for a while.

July 22 was the start of a new era for us. The tension of secrecy and anxiety about other people's reactions faded away. The need to plan, person by person, how to convey our news to each one in a considerate way was almost over. Between the two of us, we had shared every love poem we could find and every love song we could remember so far. Our confidence had increased a good deal. Now it seemed that we could begin to create the real day-to-day life we would live together these next many years. Hallelujah!

11. What kind of marriage?

Calming down a bit now, we began to take longer views. A young couple in Barbara's family was getting ready to marry, and it was interesting to think about how very different their prospects were from ours. We kind of wanted to say we were married, but the term conventionally expressed what Kate and David were planning, not what we were. A single household, merged finances, mortgage, and children were part of their married future, not ours. Gosh, some young couples six months into a romance, as we were then, were already pregnant and in line for all the challenges of child rearing. Despite the hazards, the hope of some fifty years together beckoned them. Their marriage would be nothing like ours.

So, except perhaps in private, we do not call ourselves married. We tried on many other terms and concepts—engaged, committed, partnered. We called each other "spouse" once or twice but veered instinctively away from the word "wife." Finally, we decided to call ourselves life partners. We could say "partner" for short when it was clear from the context that we didn't mean partners in business or dance or entertainment of some sort.

Living separately has some remarkable aspects to it. After many months, I still tap on the front door and/or whistle to let Barbara know I am coming in. I still do not know which drawer her silverware is in or whether she has an electric mixer. She has cleared one small drawer in her bathroom for my toiletries, but nothing else of mine stays in her house, or of hers in mine. My leaving to go home late in the evening is always hard, but we know it is right for us, and it has become a part of the full ritual we both enjoy.

For a while, Barbara worried and sometimes dreamed that, because I was "a strong and independent woman," I would get irritated by her and suddenly decide that this relationship was not for me. She was preoccupied with not being too cloying or demanding.

I could think of all kinds of traits of my own that Barbara already might not like or might slowly tire of. I wrote a little essay about it once and later showed her.

> We made a rule early on not to denigrate one another's bodies (or our own) or our behavior. Our bodies are God-given and belong to ourselves, to be treated and arrayed as each chooses. In terms of behavior, we won't sweat the small stuff, but if some behavior becomes problematic, it will be discussed in a problem-solving mode. That's the theory.

But as a result of this rule, I find that I do not know and often try to guess what things about me B might not much like, now or in the future. Perhaps she does not like my sagging eyelids, fat butt, or peacenik tattoo. Maybe she doesn't like my artwork or the amount of time it takes. Maybe she is uneasy about my having so many friends. I am so intense. When she calms me down, is it because she is a born caregiver or because she needs me to ratchet back to a level she can tolerate?

Early on she had written about this:

"I idle high," you say. I see it's true.
But me, I tick over much more slowly.
Many discoveries bind us,
but this one difference
may prove too big
even for our deepest intentions.
You know this may be so.

I am afraid we might disagree about the rightness of dying at home because I see a role for skilled nursing facilities and residential hospice. She might wrongly think I disrespect the devoted home care she provided for her mother and then her husband.

Perhaps she worries that I will resist her own wish to die at home, if it should come to that.

Perhaps she doesn't like it that I talk a lot, interrupt too much, make assumptions, don't share meals with her often, run my hand down her flank and nuzzle her neck during our morning kiss, call her darling, want sex all the time but might not be a good enough lover, am a penny pincher, don't give good gifts, and am too tall. How will I know?

My darling Barbara laughed at these anxieties and said she would tell me if anything I was doing started to bug her.

Sometimes we still worry that we do not spend enough time together to call ourselves a couple. But our daily routine is pretty normal: a quick encounter in the early morning for coffee, kisses, and plans for the day, and then two to three hours in the afternoon or evening for talk and touch. That sounds like any conventional couple, right? The difference is that we rarely share supper together unless we have guests. Is it a strange arrangement? It works for us.

Sometimes I think we will not be well tested as a couple until we have had (and made peace after) a big argument. So far, though, after a year, we haven't argued at all. Another milestone will be when one of us weeps from the core without restraint in the other's arms.

Illness or physical harm lasting more than a few days, sickness or disability that precludes sexual engagement—that will be another test for sure. Because we have both had prior experience as supportive care-givers to sick and dying people, we are pretty confident about handling that stage.

As we sort all this out, we rethink our own earlier marriages and many others we have known. We are again impressed with how much we have in common with other couples. Age makes more difference than gender. We are older and wiser, like the long-married couples nearby. People focus on making it work. There is no escape from marriage after a certain point except for the very bold. (Our friend, Nancy, at age eighty-two, after forty years of marriage, left her abusive husband in time to have one year of independent life before she died.)

People ask, and we ask ourselves, what are the hidden, subconscious motivations for falling in love, particularly late in life? Or if it just happened, what motivates you to stick with it and undertake a long-term commitment? Any man or woman committing to any man or woman could/should ask these questions:

- Are you looking for a mother or father figure? Or to be one? To replace a lost sibling?

- Do you need access to more money?
- Do you want to try something new to brighten your later years?
- Are you just hard up for sex?
- Do you want to be associated with a "better" family?
- Do you want to wean your children away from their constant claims on you by showing that you are busy with someone else?
- Do you need someone to depend upon in your old age?
- If you are lesbian or gay, do you want to prove that you can be married as well as (or better than) anyone else?
- Do you want to actively practice being a loving partner in an equal relationship?
- Do you actively want to be the survivor? *[1]

---

1 *A widowed neighbor here who, at age seventy-two or so, fell for a man ten years older, told us she explicitly wanted to test herself through the experience of caring for and then losing a partner. She had always seen this as one of the roles a full-fledged woman should have.

One perspicacious friend of mine smiled slyly and asked if I was a writer who just wanted material for a new book!

We pondered all these things while anticipating the upcoming family wedding. Young Kate and David would be asking a somewhat different set of questions and holding a different set of expectations. Still, we thought the wonderful passage on marriage in *The Prophet* by Kahlil Gibran would apply to them as well as to us. It is included at the end of this chapter.

At this wedding, I would be meeting most of Barbara's family for the first time. It was scary. Barb sent me an e-mail with details about the arrangements, and I wrote back.

> Darling, I was so in love with you already today, the work and values and lively concerns we share being so much in evidence. And then there came these wonderful details about the wedding next weekend. I am so grateful that I can be a part, very small from any public point of view but large for me. Being with you at Kate and David's wedding will quietly, almost secretly, ceremonialize my entrance into the life of your family. You will not attend as a widow but as a respected, partnered elder, and I will be seen and accepted at your side. It's a big deal, darling.

It worked out as I hoped it would. The wedding and the rest of the festivities took place on the flanks of Mt. Tamalpais. The family found us a little honeymoon cottage for two nights, close to where all the other family groups were staying. The morning of the ceremony, Barb's brothers, banned from the house where the bride and her attendants were dressing, came to share coffee and bagels with us on a deck looking over the bay.

Barbara and I participated easily in about half of the parties and rituals of the weekend. The wedding party and their guests included gay couples, old and young adults, lots of children, and people of several ethnicities from various parts of the world. They hauled chairs up to the top of the mountain for us and a couple of other elders, for that was where the ceremony took place, with the younger ones sitting on blankets on the ground.

We walked arm in arm everywhere, really needed since the ground was so rough. (Back home, too, we still do that on all possible occasions. Walking in step, my upper arm against the side of her abundant breast, fingers entwined—oh, delight!)

The issue of wedding presents is still not resolved. Barbara had found one for the young couple before she and I were really together. My inclination was to send a separate one of my own. But B said it wasn't needed, and I didn't find the right thing before the event. Of course, it is the symbolism that is at issue: Do we send a single gift as a couple, or assert our independence in situations like this? Likely we will need to sort out this kind of thing on a case by case basis. (In the end, I got the young couple a very modern kind of pitcher for Christmas.)

Since we don't usually spend the whole night together at home, our nights away at a motel or cabin are quite lovely, even though we may not sleep as well as usual. I really liked hearing the sound of the waves and feeling Barbara fall asleep, a different kind of surrender. And waking up together, already easily in one another's arms, was lovely.

Kahlil Gibran, *The Prophet*: On Marriage

Then Almitra spoke again and said, and what of
    Marriage, master? And he answered, saying:
You were born together, and together you shall be for-
    ever more. You shall be together when the white
    wings of death scatter your days. Ay, you shall be
    together even in the silent memory of God.

But let there be spaces in your togetherness,
And let the winds of the heavens dance between you.
Love one another, but make not a bond of love:
Let it rather be a moving sea between the shores of
    your souls.

Fill each other's cup but drink not from one cup.

Give one another of your bread but eat not from the
same loaf.

Sing and dance together and be joyous, but let each
of you be alone, even as the strings of the lute are
alone though they quiver with the same music.

Give your hearts, but not into each other's keeping.

For only the hand of Life can contain your hearts.

And stand together yet not too near together:

For the pillars of the temple stand apart,

And the oak tree and the cypress grow not in each
other's shadow.

12. Sex and adoration

A barrier I have wanted to overcome all my life is the "rule" from my girlhood family and friends which said that sex was a private matter (possibly somewhat naughty) and that you must not talk about it except with your (male) lover. And with him, you mostly just groped in the dark and did things without talking much about it. With a husband, in a master bedroom with the door closed, you could have the lights on and your clothes off, but you still might not talk much about what you were doing—or wished you could do.

It was OK to read about sex, and a girl was always looking for written information. There was *Masters and Johnson*, then years later *Our Bodies, Ourselves* and *The Joy of Sex* with all those explicit drawings or photographs about man-woman interactions. Eventually, there was tons of pornography on the Internet, but most of that wasn't helpful. You couldn't seem to learn anything there about caring for another person.

So you looked in novels for the sweet, sexy parts and the most explicit sections, sometimes getting a tidbit or two per book. Reading in private was more comfortable than watching the sexy scenes in movies with someone you knew sitting next to you.

Why are people in my circles so close-mouthed about the details of sexuality? Of course, we don't want to show off or make anyone uncomfortable. But we do want to learn about how to be successful sexual beings.

Long before Barbara, I wanted to share in writing my enthusiasm for love-making—always with men in those years. I wanted to write in detail about sexual experiences. I knew plenty of women would want to read that kind of stuff, maybe even some men. Sex at its best is essentially the same for all of us: kissing, touching, talking, caressing. Men can do to women everything that women can. It is only the details of penetration that are different, it seems to me. Oh, and women tend to talk about it and to stay awake afterward more easily!

But yikes, if I write in detail about what we are experiencing now, perhaps it will seem immodest or exhibitionistic. *Can I handle that? Can Barbara?*

We have decided that, except within the immediate family and circle of friends, concern about protecting our privacy or reputation is a bit old-fashioned. It is much less important than sharing what we've learned with people who want to know. Moreover, most readers will not think about us for more than a minute; rather, they will think intensely about whether these written words could apply to them.

Maybe the time is now. What have we got to lose?

First explorations

When Barbara and I literally fell together the first time, neither of us knew anything sexual about other women. Other than our mothers, perhaps, we had hardly even seen another woman naked. In ladies rooms and locker rooms, even with sisters, one stole a glance and then discreetly looked away. Our lesbian friends almost never told any sexual secrets.

I wrote a wistful poem once:

Questions for my lesbian friend

I don't need to know
how often you argue
or who pays the bills,
but I'd like to know
how you touch her breasts and
lay your body alongside hers,
how often, how slow,
what climactic orgasms you share.
Do your eyelids tingle?

How does a woman's hand feel
caressing another woman's back?
Is it not too soft, too tender,
lacking the weight and substance
that a man always brings
to my ecstasies?

Now, with Barbara, I could know for myself. I could
dare to touch her breasts, stroke her nipples, and caress
her back. Mind-blowing experiences! I was scared to kiss
her. I'd never liked the idea of kissing another woman
on the mouth, and the first time, because we were both
so shy, it felt disconcertingly soft. That changed soon
enough. We can kiss with all the full variety available to
everyone else!

Approaching the first time we would lie down
together, we both mumbled and muttered that we
wouldn't know what to do. But of course we did: it comes
naturally. It wasn't exactly because we were both women
of similar age and size and thus knew what another
woman would like. Our bodies and our responses are
considerably different in important ways. We came to
know what to do because we paid close attention to
each other, and almost from the beginning, we talked
about what we were doing and what we wanted.

Also, of course, we had both had considerable
sexual experience with men over the decades, and lots

of what you do with them is the same as you do with another woman. It feels different with a softer body and no abrasive whiskers, but kisses and caresses are familiar no matter who is giving them. The grand finale may come a different way.

At first, I worried that Barbara would miss her lost husband dreadfully at that moment. But she is a woman who lives in the present, with full appreciation for the here and now. On my part, I had a passing yearning to possess her as a man would. Soon enough, I learned how to do it my own way.

From the beginning, a major characteristic of our lovemaking was taking time—two hours, not twenty minutes. Much slow foreplay with flirting and talking and lots of time afterward, too. Is that "post-play"?

For me, looking intently at this dear woman's body was marvelously important. In the half light, the shape and shadow of her breast, her arm, her thigh, her leg—and then my arm and thigh would be there, too: oh, oh! I went through an intense spate of looking at paintings of female nudes and trying to draw. No good, never showed anyone, but it helped me learn to look.

Like the good academic researchers that we are, we reviewed *The Joy of Sex*, the *Hite Report*, and *Masters and Johnson* for anything new we could learn. Barb checked the Internet and got the advice to go slow and not focus on climax. We tried to unearth relevant lesbian literature and found very little in the beginning. In three novels, the plot was about a lesbian woman wooing and winning a straight woman, and a lesbian friend told us that's almost always the way it happens, not two straight women suddenly coming together.

There was a good book by sex therapist Glenda Corwin, who advocated, among other things, "twenty-four-hour foreplay." That suited my obsession with Barbara's strong substantial legs, which has me stroking them with mine, or with my hands or with my feet, on all possible occasions, clothed or not.

Theoretically, we were willing to just play around without "going for the Full Tamasha," as we call it. (That's the Urdu word for *celebration*.) But half-measures didn't suit either of us.

Agreements

Very early on, we established those general understandings we've already described, mostly about avoiding things like perfume and lipstick, sex toys, and too much product in our hair.

When planning to lie down together, we also have to take whatever preventative measures we need to keep from coughing, getting leg cramps, suffering from acid reflux, whatever. We laugh at these old-age problems to keep from being embarrassed about them.

On the other hand, age disappears most amazingly once you lie down. Lying in the half light, clothes and glasses off, having learned where to look and where to move my hands, I experience Barbara as twenty years younger than she really is. Her face is younger yet at some angles. And I myself am ageless. No erogenous zone appears to have lost responsivity. When you are lying down with the endorphins pumping, your hips and knees suddenly don't hurt at all.

Figuring out how often to lie down together took some exploration. Of course, we would both have to want it at the same time—that led to some dithering, as we each tried to figure out if the other was eager or not before revealing her own proclivities. A couple of times a week generally seems to work well.

We keep trying new things. I assume that means that she, like me, spends time alone pondering the possibilities. I sometimes put my hands on my own body to think through how best to touch hers. It remains hard to believe how turned on we both are. And there is our wonderful propensity to humor—to be flirtatious and mischievous, to laugh and giggle, in bed and out. When you are really happy, it is easy to be silly and giddy.

Perfect stage of life

Repeatedly, we congratulate one another on how easy sexual romance is at this age. For starters, we are more confident in ourselves than young people can be, and we are sexually experienced. Moreover, we don't have to worry about menstruation, pregnancy, venereal disease, interruption by crying babies or curious children. Neither of us has to leave the conjugal bed for a job or is too distracted by obligations at home or away. We have privacy any hour of the day or night. Infidelity is not a concern; neither of us is likely to be pursued by someone else at this age! We have no major reputation to protect. This is a great age and stage of life for any romance. And for two women together, California in 2018 was a highly desirable time and place in history.

We do each still worry that the other will become irritated, disillusioned, or overburdened at some point. We can't believe anyone could be attracted to what we see in our own mirrors. So we don't look there much, each preferring instead to be charmed by the other.

24/7 foreplay

Like new lovers of every sort, and perhaps like all wise lovers of every age and variety, Barbara and I are into 24/7 foreplay, as you might call it. Glenda Corwin, in her book on sexual intimacy among women, introduced the concept, but she did not give a very clear description of the kisses and caresses, compliments, cards, sweet remarks in person and by e-mail—how you can keep all that coming all day long so that when the time arrives for your evening rendezvous, both of you are eager for it. The tidy room, attractive bed, clean sheets, and filtered light are part of foreplay, really. What you wear and how you take it off—well, you know how the bedroom scene is supposed to play out. We just try to remember that what happens in the morning and during the day is part of preparing for that private time later.

Orgasm

Orgasm is very different for me with Barbara than it was with a guy or is when I am on my own. Discovering such a thing is mind-blowing. Orgasm was so pinpointed and clitoral for me when I was with a man. I have a different kind of genital experience now, but also, more amazingly, there is often a cataclysmic full-body response. *What is this? Do people know about this?*

It took many months to find anything like it described in the Hite Report, sex therapist writings, or anyone's novel. Feeling Barbara's inner geography with my finger, I sometimes wonder: Can a male penis distinguish and delight in these protuberances and valleys?

The men I knew never said. After such delight and response, I hardly need Barbara to bring me off in turn, though she always does.

Although the full-body response on my part already provides a kind of mutual orgasm, sometimes we yearn to reach genital orgasm together, both coming at the same time, to dramatize our deep root connection. But the sex therapists we read point out that heterosexual partners also often do not climax together and perhaps reach greater satisfaction when they do not. Focusing on the moves that will lead to your own climax distracts substantially from pleasing your partner. So going one at a time often makes more sense, from a generous emotional point of view as well as physiologically. Nevertheless, as we all know, when it happens that, in one way or another, you both climax at once, it feels great.

Barbara and I can talk—in advance, during, and after—about these things in a freer way than I remember ever doing with a man. But perhaps I was simply not assertive enough back in those days. I loved sex with men, but I know I always followed the guy's lead. I hoped but did not ask for what I wanted.

There is another wonderful thing. Barb and I are both ambidextrous in love making. Either one of us can tend sweetly and deeply to the other with either the left or the right hand. We take turns on the two sides of the bed, facing the dimmed light or away, seeing a new side of the other from what we gazed at two days ago. Oh!

Refinements

We go for it in the daytime, too, sometimes by prior arrangement and sometimes on the spur of the moment. Here's part of an e-mail I wrote to Barb at noon one day:

> This is what we get when we stay significantly apart more than forty-eight hours, right? The totally irrational yearning for close physical contact ASAP! Can I come at 3:30?
>
> How has it happened that I, a woman who lived by choice for twenty-three recent years without meaningful physical contact with anyone (even my grandchildren were not available for cuddling) am now foisting myself upon you like a teenager?! Can I come at 3:30?

Most of the time, I wash up at home and remove all but a minimum of clothes before I walk the back way to her place, and she greets me just barely dressed herself. One or the other of us may have been planning some new way to start, to lie, to kiss, to touch—the butterfly, the circles in or out from points of interest, stroking six inches from here to there, the backs of knees, the inner elbow. Or let's just flop diagonally across the bed or lie end to end: I love her legs so much.

We no longer feel stiff or lame once we lie down. We know where to look and how to adore (not ignore) the lesser attributes. A half-teaspoon of the "long-lasting personal lubrication" is in the little cup by the bed, easy to scoop up on a fingertip. But half the time, there's no need to use it.

Of course, really good mutual lovemaking is very similar for everyone, whatever the age and gender. The tensions and obligations of the world, ego, and personality fall away entirely. There comes that deep sense of listening to the other; it is really both listening and feeling for every nuance of response, an I-Thou focus that feels almost divine. The opportunity to hide oneself in the other for a few moments, however one does it, is a moment of deep emotional respite, a true blessing.

Restoration

We stay together a long time after reaching the high point, petting and patting, stroking and talking another hour. Gazing long into one another's eyes after words fail is "the greatest marvel man possesses," according to Milan Kundera. Once in a while, we fall asleep for a few moments together, and often we halfway yearn to stay together all night. But we mostly only do that when we are away from home. People as old as we are suffer too many interruptions to sleep. So I drag myself away from her, finally, put on those few clothes, and walk the back way to my apartment. Once I am out and on my way, it is a lovely little walk in the dark. There is an element of self-reclamation in going back to my own lone table, bed, and book. It is not lonely. It is a way of restoring myself for the next time.

Barbara also has a little post-coital ritual that I love. When finally we rise from lying together, especially if I go into the other room at that point, Barb will remake the bed with its spare masculine colors and lines and turn down the covers on one side, her side, ready for her return there after I leave. I know that this ritual is part of her reclaiming herself after the give-away of lovemaking.

Expecting change

Barbara hopes we will remain orgasmic until our dying days and revels in the fact that this seems more possible for women than for men. I tend to expect that some kind of illness or disability eventually will preclude "the Full Tamasha." As wrinkles, age-marks, and bruises overcome us, we might gaze admiringly at one another less often. But the delights of bare-skin touch—stroke, caress, kiss, and fondle—will surely be available to us to the end. The deepest intimacy of sex is not in orgasm but in offering one's naked vulnerability to the other. The outside world disappears. The sense of being bodily and spiritually bonded and blessed becomes the main reward.

I have a perverse desire to be a better lover than the men in Barbara's life but have vowed never really to ask. If this were better for her, would that make her a lesbian in her own eyes? It is not like that for me. Sex with my husband, and better yet with my lover of twelve years, was beyond fabulous. Those super orgasms—OMG!

But the loving, personal, heart-meeting compatibility I find with Barbara is beyond compare to anything I have known before.

I am still so much in love with this woman. How could this have lasted a whole year, this marvel? Is it slightly narcissistic? Maybe it is! We are so much alike—but also such different personalities. It is our great good luck.

13. Growing appreciation

We are always looking for ways to express the swirl of romantic feelings. Barbara finds little gifts and cards for me all the time. I keep on writing poems.

Bosom Buddies

In the waking, walking, working hours of the day,
I sometimes cannot remember you
the way you are,
the lush press of your bosom against mine,
the tangled legs, the searching mouth,
the reaching fingers and rising hips.

I haven't remembered,
so it's new again,
every time.

Still, once in a while, a moment of panic or doubt will occur for one of us. *Can we do this? Will we live long enough? What is "long enough"? Will I lose her? Will I survive OK afterward?*

Two nights running, I have more or less the same dream. I've gone to a party or a committee meeting and can't find my car when I come out in the dark. I walk up and down several blocks, back and forth, looking for my car. Suddenly, having walked so far, I realize I am looking for the wrong car. I've been watching for my old red Honda, the one I traded in for the "silver pine" Prius just the week before I first lay down with Barbara.

I take from this dream that, at deep levels, I am still sorting out my identity. *Who am I? Can you hold all that I am? How much should I keep back and why? To protect my own privacy? My soul? To protect you?*

When you are in love with someone, it is because you want your ultimate aloneness to be breached, to be healed. But that can never be completely accomplished during a human lifetime. So how do you handle that? One tries and tries.

We have agreed to go for broke as far as sex is concerned—yes, yes—as much and as often as we can while the going is good. This includes trying everything we can think of, every which way. We studied *The Joy of Sex* again, Susan Quilliam's revised version. Despite all the many erect penises in the pictures, there is lots in that book for a female couple to learn about the possibilities.

All sex researchers since 1970 agree that female orgasm results from direct or indirect clitoral stimulation and that the infamous internal "G Spot" does not have to be reached for orgasm to occur. It is interesting for us to read generalizations about the female body and then figure out which ideas actually apply to us. Not all women are alike, and there are substantial differences between the two of us. The song in my head is, "Getting to know you, getting to know all about you."

What is the purpose of love and lust for us old ones, we ask each other. Reproduction has nothing to do with it, and the old "biological imperative" should have expired long ago. Is there any evolutionary advantage to engaging in sexual activity in old age? Is it good for the ego, the psyche, the soul? Or is it just a residual habit, quick to surface again when the opportunity arises? Does libido increase with practice? Do our hormone levels change? *Am I sprouting more hairs on my chin?*

At this point, Barbara is likely to suggest that I am over-thinking the whole thing and that I should just lie still and pay attention to her hands. She has slowly led me further and further past my residual resistances so that I can open my body and heart to her.

I know that none of us are quite as we seem to others. On the whole, I appear strong and competent. But I don't like Barbara to say admiring things about me. I need her to be one of the very few who know how volatile I really am, how deeply I can doubt myself.

Barbara also is seen as a stalwart leader among people here, appreciated for being well-organized, reliable in follow-through on commitments, a good writer, introducing activities that promote community life. Only I know the mischievous bright eyes and dazzling smile she can show in bed. Only I am aware of her indecisiveness in personal matters sometimes and how last-minute changes of plan can dismay her.

I am a more relaxed partner than I was in my twenties. I remember often being embarrassed in public by the man who was my husband so many decades ago. Even then, I knew I was overly identifying myself with him so that I thought it reflected upon me when he was inconsiderate or bombastic in public. After all, I had chosen him, right?

Fifty years later, I am more mature and independent. Maybe I could still be embarrassed by some accidental gaffe of Barb's, but watching her in public now, I am just curious. We remain clearly separate people. I am pleased but not proud or proprietary about her accomplishments. Wouldn't that be patronizing? I don't own her accomplishments or her.

When I was twenty-six, if my husband dozed off on the chair next to me in public, I would be irritated and embarrassed. If Barbara drowses during our quiet church service, I am just fond and accepting: I know how little sleep she got during the last busy days. If she starts to make her darling little falling-asleep noises, I just press my foot against hers to rouse her.

Oh, I love this lady. Let me write here the long-promised list of things that I love about her.

1. Barbara is large, almost as tall as I and heavier. I could never interact so comfortably with the body of a smaller woman.

2. I love her glowing eyes, her shining hair, her smile, her laugh, her breasts, her legs, and particularly her flanks.

3. I like the way Barbara decorates and keeps tidy her rooms, how much she reads, the music she listens to (many kinds), and how she keeps up with the news.

4. I like her decisiveness—and the contrasting moments of dither, mostly caused by not yet knowing my preferences.

5. I like the way she promptly answers calls and e-mails, appears on time, and follows up promptly on decisions and cues. She is responsible and responsive.

6. I like Barbara's clothes—proper, informal, and negligee—and her jewelry.

7. I very much appreciate her devotion to her family of origin and to her husband's relatives and offspring. I very much like

what I have seen of her brothers and their wives and children. I am honored by the way she has introduced me to all these people and how they have welcomed me.

8. She values and supports all my family relationships as well and wants to be friends with all my people. She has no inclination to jealousy.

9. I should have put sense of humor at the top of this list, and honesty, modesty, and intelligence.

10. Or maybe topmost should be Barbara's libido and stamina, astonishing at her age, in my view.

11. I love her creativity, responsiveness, flexibility, and good humor as a lover. We laugh about so much so often.

12. Barb has a good and clear mind, always helpful to a relationship. She can pay attention, remember what she's learned, interpret what she sees in me, and imagine what I am feeling.

13. It is crucial and basic to our relationship that each of us is committed to the long-term well-being of this cooperative

community and its individual members, residents, and staff. Barbara takes on her full share of community work.

14. Barbara and I are learning a huge amount from this unexpected adventure. I adore her flexibility, patience, and willingness to learn.

15. It is marvelous how supportive she is of this writing project.

16. I am grateful that she is even more steadfast than I about our decision to live separately, even though she was so long accustomed to living with a husband.

17. Barbara fulfills my deepest dream, long ago abandoned, of having a life partner who is intelligent, mature, and ready to share on an equal footing with me in responding to life's delights and vicissitudes.

I admire and adore this woman!

On July 10, at 2 in the morning, she wrote a little love note, long-hand on paper.

> Maybe it seems to you that I take what has happened in these last four months just matter-of-factly. But underneath, if I'm honest with myself, I am absolutely staggered by how you have changed my life so completely.

I am in your hands, my dearest—and it seems that you are in mine. Equal parts joy and terror! But overlaid with commitment and determination to move ahead—with you.

Me, too! Yup, I am planning to keep her!

14. The books we read

During this revolutionary year, being the academic researchers that we are, Barbara and I read whatever we could get hold of to help us understand what was happening to us.

Looking for novels about late life romance between two women, books based on real life and well written, we found a number. We liked these best.

> *Desert of the Heart,* Jane Rule, (Bella Books, 1964). This early classic of lesbian literature describes a growing romance between a young lesbian and a straight woman fifteen years her senior in Reno and Pyramid Lake in Nevada.

> *This is Not for You,* Jane Rule, (Insomniac Press, 2005). Towards the end of her years as a prominent lesbian leader in Canada, and after publishing nine other books, Rule wrote this somewhat abstruse "letter" to a partner from whom she had separated.

Prism, Valerie Taylor, (Naiad Press, 1981). Like Jane Rule, Valerie Taylor was a leader in the lesbian community and wrote several books. This novel describes how a lesbian woman slowly and gently "awakens" a straight woman, in this case both over the age of sixty.

Night Lights, Bonnie Shrewsbury Arthur, (Mother Courage Press, 1987). Bonnie was a neighbor of mine when I first came here. Her novel also is about a lesbian woman, a young grandmother who falls for the unhappy heterosexual divorcee next door and slowly figures out how to approach her forthrightly.

Nonfiction sex studies of various sorts are available. We were particularly impressed to realize how relevant these books are no matter what sexual predisposition the reader might have.

The Hite Report, Shere Hite, (Dell Press, 1976). This path-breaking study is famous for documenting that female orgasm is not dependent upon accessing some mythological G-Spot deep in the vagina but is almost always dependent upon clitoral stimulation—by penis, fingers, mouth, tongue, or perhaps vibrator. Note that this means the size of penis is not important and the ability to maintain an erection is not crucial to satisfying a woman. No woman needs to strap on a dildo to satisfy another woman.

Masters and Johnson on Sex and Human Loving, William Masters, Virginia Johnson, & Robert Kolodny, (Little Brown, 1982). Straightforward classic overview of almost everything known at the time about sexuality. See especially chapter 9 on "Love" and chapter 17, "Increasing sexual satisfaction."

The Joy of Sex, Revised, Alex Comfort and Susan Quilliam, (Three Rivers Press, 2008). This updated revision of a 1972 book that has sold more than 12 million copies worldwide is instructive for women even though all of its dramatic photographs and drawings feature a man and a woman together. After all, everything a man can do with his mouth, his fingers, his thumb, and his big toe (!); with his arms, legs, feet, tongue, eyelashes, etc., a woman also can do for her female partner.

For Yourself: The Fulfillment of Female Sexuality, Lonnie Garfield Barbach, (Anchor Books, 1975 and 2000). Detailed instructions about masturbation and how to become orgasmic. Assumes male partners but would work with a female partner also.

Books about late-life romances mostly report on heterosexual couples, with a token chapter or two about gay people. But, of course, almost all of it applies to all of us, whether we are gay or straight—or something else, like Barb and me!

Late Life Loves: Romance and Relationships in Later Years, Connie Goldman, (Fairview Press, 2006). Formerly on the NPR staff, Goldman interviewed twenty-two couples involved in late-life romances. Some have married; others have deliberately avoided marriage. Some live together; some deliberately do not. The pros and cons are cheerfully discussed.

Older Couples: New Romances, Edith and Jerrold Kemp, (Celestial Arts, 2002). As it says on the back cover, this book "challenges our stereotypes about aging and intimacy. Focusing on the issues faced by single, divorced and/or widowed seniors, [it] offers inspirational as well as practical advice for finding, attracting, and maintaining a loving partnership in later life."

The New Love and Sex After 60, Dr. Robert Butler and Myrna Lewis, (Ballantine Books, 2002). Butler is the Grand Old Man of aging and sexuality in America. This updated edition of the 1976 original presents researched medical data in an easily readable style. There's a lot about medical problems, especially erectile dysfunction, but emotional and social challenges are also discussed.

Seasons of the Heart: Love, Sex and Romance after 60, Zenith H. Gross, (New World Library, 2000). This affirming book quotes many elders and cites many other useful books. There is a full-fledged chapter on same-sex couples and their late-life romantic experiences.

Undefended Love, Jett Psaris and Marlena Lyons, (New Harbinger, 2000). Knowing that men and women alike at some level yearn to open themselves to emotional intimacy with others, the authors talk about how we can change ourselves in ways that will make that more possible.

Specifically relevant for two women loving and living together:

Sexual Intimacy for Women: A Guide for Same-Sex Couples, Dr. Glenda Corwin, (Seal Press, 2010). A clinical psychologist specializing in female same-sex couples, Dr. Corwin has offered a very useful book to "help women overcome common issues around orgasm, body image, identity, aging and parenthood."

Lesbian Sex, JoAnn Loulan (Bookpeople, 1984). Very useful discussion of most of the challenges involved in lesbian sexuality.

The Coming Out Stories, edited by Julia Stanley and Susan Wolfe, (Persephone Press, 1980). This is a poignant collection of forty stories about the hardship suffered by many lesbians as they struggled to come out in California in the seventies. Being straight all our lives and falling for one another only as elders in 2018, Barbara and I never experienced such hostilities or had to overcome such hurdles. Hats off to those others who helped to pave the way for us!

Books we (re)read about mature loving relations with no emphasis on sexuality or sexual orientation including some old classics from college days:

I and Thou, Martin Buber, (Scribner and Sons, 1970). This second edition of the classic 1958 original includes an introduction by Walter Kaufmann, which is very helpful in sorting out Buber's abstruse style.

The Art of Loving, Erich Fromm, (Harper, 1956). Fromm rails against western materialism and talks in detail about how we could become more loving. The basic elements common to all forms of love, he claims, are "care, responsibility, respect and knowledge."

The Third Force: The Psychology of Abraham Maslow, Frank Goble, (Viking Adult, 1970). Like Buber and Fromm, Maslow reached for the most evolved and mature in people, sharing his insights into how we can be at our best in the world and in relation to others.

Androgyny has been a fascination of mine for two decades, but I have not found much in the literature. Suggestions are welcome!

> *Androgyny: Toward a New Theory of Sexuality,* June Singer, (Anchor Press, 1976). Some chapters in this book were useful for understanding the nature of androgyny and its place in the mature psyche.

Caregiving, dying, and death are likely to come to the forefront in our relationship before we're done, so we will read a lot on those subjects. No book is likely to impress us more than Sallie Tisdale's.

> *Advice for Future Corpses (and Those Who Love Them),* Sallie Tisdale, (Simon & Schuster, 2018). We went step by step together through this blunt and detailed book about being an effective caregiver for a dying partner. We think everyone over fifty in America should read it, and we bought copies for lots of our friends.

One more: a fascinating demographic study caught our attention.

> *Going Solo: The Extraordinary Rise and Surprising Appeal of Living Alone*, by Eric Klinenberg, (Penguin, 2012).

15. Traveling in America

Riding the train

Finally the time came in mid-October for us to take Amtrak's California Zephyr across the country to Chicago and then the Capitol Limited on to Washington, DC. We thought of it as a honeymoon trip, and the overnight in Chicago surely was. But the train itself posed a number of challenges.

First of all, before we even got on the train, we worried about how we would be leaving open-minded California and might be identified and shunned as female lovers. No such thing happened, but the irony was that we ourselves looked hard at other women traveling together: "Those two don't look in the least like sisters; do you think they really are?"

We travelled in a sleeping compartment, far more expensive but in many ways not really preferable to coach, I thought, having earlier tripped across the country several times alone. In coach, the upholstered, reclining seats are much more comfortable than the bench seats in the compartment. At night, your body is aligned with the direction the train is moving, which seemed to make the rumble and roll easier to adapt to than when lying on a bunk crosswise to the direction of the train. On the other hand, in our private compartment, some of the time we could lie together, which was lovely, of course. And in the sleeping car, the bathroom is on the same level, you can actually take a shower, and there is free coffee.

It was new for us to spend the full day and night together, but we managed very well, bickering mildly only about who would laboriously climb up into the upper bunk. We soaked up the passing scenery and talked about everything under the sun. We hardly read the books we had brought and never got out the playing cards.

We ate all meals in the dining car. Every time, we were placed with new, random tablemates and shared the usual banal conversations. One or two of those would have been enough for me.

Meanwhile, though, gorgeous views of American villages and farms streamed past our windows, with the deep red-rock gorges of the Colorado River being the prime exhibit in the middle of the route.

In Chicago, Barbara splurged on the most elegant hotel suite I have ever been in, on the eighteenth floor of the Blackstone Hotel with a huge window overlooking Lake Shore Drive with its huge statuesque buildings and the curved bay of Lake Michigan. Enormous beds, marble bathroom fixtures, mirrors, and paintings! Barbara insisted that we should enjoy such occasional luxuries now while the going is good. We were not likely to make such a trip again. The Art Institute was just down the street, and we spent a morning there before we went back to the station to catch the Capitol Limited to Washington.

Visiting relatives

This was a year of meeting all sorts of new people for both of us, of course, and in D.C., I took Barbara to meet and stay over that first night with my second sister and her husband. Behind the cordial meet and greet, everyone was wondering about what impression we would make on one another. Myrina's husband was failing mentally, and watching them together was sobering for Barbara and me, as we have undertaken the risk of sharing such disabilities ourselves at some point in the future.

Mostly, though, we had a good time. In the basement guest room of Myrina's house, not having figured out the lights, Barbara and I entwined ourselves together in total darkness, a wonderfully surreal experience I would like to repeat some time. The next day, while Michael was at an adult day care center, we went with Myrina to the Native American Museum, one of the most well-designed, attractive museums I have seen. Barb left us after that and headed west again.

Myrina and I spent several days together in between her excursions away, and another sister came down from upstate New York to visit. I encouraged them to ask about Barb and me, though they were reticent. Emily thought I would be "different," but I really am not, except perhaps for being more affectionate toward everyone, an overflow of my feelings for Barb. Myrina tried out referring to me as lesbian, and I explained why I don't relate to that term, even though it turns out that I can enjoy a woman's body as much as I did for so long enjoy the bodies of men. (*Could I/would I enjoy sexual engagement with a man now?*)

On the whole, it may be that my family people are more impressed by the idea that I could fall in love with anyone at all than they are interested in who it is. I am so independent and self-determined a woman in their eyes that this is a new me from their point of view. Living 3,000 miles away from my family of origin all my adult life, I have not generally revealed my considerable vulnerabilities to them or told them of the previous times I have been quite infatuated with one guy or another. But now I am more open and try to convey to my sisters that now, finally, I have found the equal adult partner I had always dreamed of.

At the Episcopal church, Myrina and Michael, who are well known there, were greeted most tenderly by other parishioners, and I, too, by extension, was welcomed very warmly. The service reminded me that many Christian concepts are no longer relevant or useful for me. But golly, the Mozart *Ave Maria*, not the words but the music itself, brought tears from deep within me. Sometimes I have this numinous sense, both joyful and heartbroken, of being able to "confront the mystery of existence," as a Zen author has said. But it might just be emotional, and most others don't know what I am talking about. It doesn't matter.

I had agreed to stay with Michael while Myrina made several short visits to friends and family. I am quite fond of Mike, and we managed well together. But by my tenth day in D.C., I was suddenly horribly homesick and wished I could go home at once. Should old ladies get homesick? I hated being separated so many days from my own true love! But I had freely volunteered for this stint, so soon enough, the song in my head was "Take my life and let it be/consecrated, Lord, to thee." (I still sing hymns like this even though I now consider myself a religious post-theist.)

Barbara's trip

Speaking of last-chance travels, while I settled down with Michael so that my sister could take some days away, Barbara flew off to visit friends and destinations across the country. The last half of her trip involved driving alone some 1,200 miles over five days, from New Mexico to Sacramento.

At her first stop in Cincinnati, Barb visited old friends. Then she moved on to Yellow Springs and Antioch College, old stomping grounds for her. One of her overnights was an AirBnB rental in one of those new tiny houses.

She flew on to Albuquerque and then drove alone, four to five driving hours per day for five days across deserts and through mountains. A solo long-distance driver myself in my younger days, I was impressed. Her notes give a glimpse of how it was.

- Chimayo: Ortega weavers.

- Abiquiu to Durango: brilliant fall yellows, high elevation meadows, deer.

- Durango to Grand Junction: another spectacular drive.

- Colorado Rockies: alpine views, snow on peaks, and right at the side of the road in

the high passes at 11,000 feet. Hairpin
turns and switchbacks, timber line.

- Evidence of old mining sites; Silverton;
  red rock canyons.

- Grand Junction: California Zephyr in
  the night. Public art all around town.

- Final dash: Salt Lake City, Elko, Reno.

- "Big sky" continues, but now the land-
  scape is pastel high desert, bleached sage,
  and tumbleweed, old mesas and hills,
  gorgeous clouds.

Why did I do this? I love to fly; why didn't
I just fly straight back to Sacramento? Or
stay with E. in DC? To prove to myself that
I could. As with the London trip last year,
both to reclaim and to say goodbye. To fill
the time while E. was away.

What an adventurer! Barbara is not spry, but she
is a careful planner, which is what made this trip safe, I
guess. Still, I was glad to be learning how to text so that
I could reassure myself that she was OK. In turn, she
worried about me often having to go up and down two
flights of stairs in Michael's house. (We have none at all
at home, and they are hard for me.) What if he or I fell?

It was those stairs—two flights—that caused Barbara to panic when she couldn't reach me one evening. She imagined me fallen and helpless. Her concern made me feel a bit crowded and cloistered at first. I am not used to having to worry about people who might be worried about me; no one has for forty years. I have learned to be independent and, in many ways, invisible and have quite liked it. Now, with Barbara, I am closely watched, seen to the core, and much less alone. I am slowly learning to like this, too, but it is a process.

Despite my intermittent concerns and contacts by text and phone, much of the time Barbara was out of sight and out of mind for me even though I love her well. This was disconcerting. It happens at home sometimes, too. Having been totally independent for so long, of course, I can be so still. I want this to be a reassurance to Barbara and myself, because one of us will be alone again in the foreseeable future. If she dies first, I know I will manage OK. But it feels a little disloyal sometimes.

While she was out there on the long highways, Barbara made up a list of things she most likes about me.

A few things I love about Elizabeth:

The way she...

- makes everyone she talks with feel special.

- reaches out even to those who are hard to love.

- is willing to try anything once.

- interrogates her motives and holds herself responsible.

- looks for the good in people and is slow to criticize.

- is creative.

- supports her children, grandchildren, and sisters.

- has been a staunch and faithful member of her women's group.

- gives the most erotic, feathery kisses.

- likes to weave our legs together.

- is a voracious reader.

- is so bright and intellectually curious.

- writes poetry! loves to sing! to drum! to dance! to make art!

- the way she responded to my families,
  Benham and Tye;

and

her boisterous, wholehearted laughs and whoops;
her distinctive fashion style;
her eyes;
how she makes me feel loved.

16. Still not marrying

Valentine's Day has new meaning now. But Barb said to just write her a silly verse. So I did.

> There was an old woman named Tye,
> whom nobody would have called spry,
> but her lover has said
> once you got her to bed,
> what she did there was perfectly fine.

I gave her the rhyme along with a flower. She gave me a gorgeous card and a box of ginger chocolates. We sat facing one another on my convertible couch with my stockinged foot inquisitively between her legs. She said she was "smitten"; I said I was "in thrall." We laughed over nothing, and then we laughed again. We've been together almost a year. I thought "in love" never lasted beyond six months. I wonder if I can get her into bed this shining afternoon.

As our time together approached a year, and we were still saying we were not going to get married in the conventional sense, we got a new set of questions and complaints from people.

"But we want to know what marriage means for you or what this is if it doesn't fit under that name," a younger woman urged.

"We want to be able to bless and celebrate your union," a sister-in-law protested.

"I'm in love, too, Mom," my middle-aged daughter said, "and I am partly looking to you as a model for whether to marry again."

It was easy enough to explain again why we didn't need a wedding. We didn't feel the need for a church blessing, wedding presents, or an expensive party. We didn't want to call attention to ourselves or to be in the limelight. Big gatherings can be overwhelming, especially for me.

In my jaded view, weddings, even in the good old days, involved bribing an innocent young girl into a life of obligation and servitude with a pretty dress, a lot of presents, a cake, and a big party. Nowadays, weddings involve outrageously expensive destination trips intended more to attract the maximum number of casual friends than to invoke the blessings of the immediate family. These extravaganzas compete for glamour and originality with other such weddings and distract badly from the mutual commitment that was once thought to be the main point. Barbara and I are not drawn to participate in this wedding culture.

Regarding legal marriage itself, our associates readily got it that we didn't need to combine our finances for mutual support and that we don't want to complicate things for our heirs.

But it was more challenging to think through for ourselves and then explain to others about not sharing a household. Are we just "friends with benefits" or "full-service friends," as the young ones might put it? We like having our separate places, but sometimes each of us yearns to be at home with the other for hours, nights, or days at a time. We sometimes fret that not sharing money, food, and housekeeping (or children, of course) makes our union too easy. *Is marriage only "real" when it is difficult?*

In my women's group, we played with the idea that the trouble with marriage was mainly that men are so obtuse! But soon, we concluded that it is cohabitation itself that is always so challenging.

If Barb and I lived together, there could be the danger of slipping into the conventional roles of man and wife. Instead of each taking full care of her own apartment, interior decoration, finances, transportation, shopping, food preparation, and garden space, we might fall into a division of labor that imitated the man-woman roles of the old-time household. We'd be likely to divide up the tasks just to avoid disagreements. We might become too dependent upon one another, even as we know one of us will probably have to go it alone later.

Once early on, I totally panicked with the fear that I would totally lose myself if I moved in with Barbara or got too close to her. What if, in response to her natural mothering instincts, I became too much like a kid again?

Barbara likes to shop, buys better ingredients for meals, and cooks better than I do—it would be hard not to let her take the lead there. I have strong feelings about how a space is decorated, lit, and maintained. We have differing inclinations regarding entertaining, gardening, and driving.

Barbara and I eat different kinds of things at different times of day, partially for health reasons that cannot be avoided. She likes music playing much of the time; I mostly prefer silence. I make off-beat paintings and found-object mobiles, which she might well not want on her walls. Both of us treasure having a lot of time alone. Both of us suffer from sleep disturbances which would be doubly problematic if we knew they were disrupting a sleeping partner as well.

I entertain individuals at many hours of day (including overnight) and groups of people (including my women's group, a worship sharing group, a drum circle, a painters' salon, and a book group) that Barbara is not part of. Imagine if we shared an apartment, and she had to somehow get out of the way when these visitors were present! I suppose I could give these groups up or arrange for them all to be hosted elsewhere. But we have agreed that we don't want to stop being the person with whom the other first fell in love.

Despite these impediments, Barbara and I probably would move in together and figure out these challenges if our apartments were blocks or miles apart. But it takes about three minutes to walk from my front door to hers. No driving required. No finding a parking space. This senior community—ANY elder community—is the perfect place to live in a close, committed relationship while still maintaining separate households.

We do sometimes wonder if, lacking the conventional challenges (children, money, household, upward mobility), we will get bored with ourselves—after we have caught up on fifty separate years of adult life, that is! There again, the retirement community environment is advantageous. We both are very involved in supporting our more fragile neighbors, the community programs, and our worship group. There are constant changes and challenges on all sides: plenty to talk about, new people to know, and new things to learn all the time.

17. Ring ceremony

Yikes, we avoided a fancy big wedding, but even our little ring ceremony took a huge amount of planning. We shopped around and eventually ordered our rings many weeks in advance. Wrought in silver, they feature two strands looped together, like our lives. We figured out our guest list, drafted out the ceremony and the celebration for afterward, reserved guest rooms, planned food, bought champagne, on and on. *Oh, gosh, what should I wear?*

We can't easily seat more than eight people in our living rooms, so we invited only six guests, three each. Our guests were important to us, but extraneous circumstances played a role, too, and we knew we were leaving out some people who would have loved to be with us. We welcomed their blessings from afar.

We set our ceremony for March 2, our first anniversary as a couple. My daughter and her new man came from an hour away. For my daughter, it was also a reunion with a dear lesbian friend of mine who had first known her when she was fourteen and seen her only once since then. Barbara's three old friends and academic colleagues from southern California drove up and spent the weekend.

Barb and I each hosted a luncheon for our small group of four. Ten minutes before my guests arrived, I was nervous as a bride. *Was I supposed to put the avocado into the pasta or into the salad? Should I offer a toast to Marlane, who knew my daughter long ago?* It all went smoothly.

Then, at the appointed time, Barb's "wedding party" came to my apartment, where my group welcomed them with huzzas and cameras. Everyone met and mingled for a little while; then we settled down for our short ceremony, all sitting in a circle in my living room.

Barbara and I were adapting, at a minimalist level, a traditional Quaker marriage process. It was my role to explain how these six dear ones had, along with others, all unwittingly served as our "serial clearness committee."

> During those early months, we shared with you what was happening to us, informally "testing" for your reactions. You helped assure us that we were "clear" to go forward with our commitment to one another.

I reminded them that, as they knew already, this would be a slightly different kind of marriage—not legalized, not sharing money or home, the two of us being both committed and independent. Similarly, we were having a different kind of wedding, not one big expensive party but a series of small observations.

March 2: I told them that March 2 one year ago was the first date of record, the day we first really understood that we belonged together from that time on.

June 6: Then Barb explained how she had already removed her wedding ring and invoked her husband, Ken, who had died three years previous. "We betrothed ourselves to one another on June 6, in a ceremony on the Kunde hilltop, at which I asked Ken to release me to Elizabeth. With only Ken as a witness, we sat knee to knee and promised ourselves to one another until death should part us."

July 22: I told that on July 22, in a much-adapted version of a regular Quaker wedding ceremony, we stood before our peers in the Friends House Worship Group and declared ourselves to be a couple.

October: Barb explained that in October, both of us were starting to feel the need for a visible symbol of our mutual commitment, and we started looking for a ring that we would both like to wear. We found a good choice in December and ordered this ring in January.

March 2 again, today: It was my turn to explain that this was the anniversary of the date we first understood ourselves to be in love with one another. As Barbara had taken off her wedding ring, I had removed from the fourth finger of my left hand the ring symbolizing "balance" that I had worn for at least twenty years. Maybe that was meaningful: Barbara's presence in my life had indeed shifted the balance. We have gained a new equilibrium now.

We invited questions and remarks. Then:

Barb: OK, now we will exchange these rings with our pledge to one another. First, we will gather ourselves in silence for a few minutes. Then, Elizabeth and I will ceremoniously open the jewelry box, speak to each other saying what this means to us, and put a ring upon the other's ring finger. Another bit of grateful silence will follow; then let's clasp hands around the circle.

We settled into a gathering silence, breathing deep and feeling the intention of the moment. Barbara opened the elegant box with the rings and put one on my finger. Ooooh, I was glad!

> Barbara: Dear Elizabeth, my totally unexpected late-life love, my new life partner for as long as we may have, whether one year or ten, and whatever challenges may lie ahead—I am proud and joyful to share it with you. I will always carry you in my heart.

Then it was my turn to put the ring on her finger.

> Elizabeth: My darling Barbara, at a time when I thought I had all I needed and wanted, at a time when I thought I knew myself well, you came as an overwhelming astonishment into my life, into my bed, and into my heart.
>
> I have learned so much about you and about myself in this last year. We know now the limitations and the potential of our late-life commitment. I intend to be your loving partner, joyful and steadfast at your side, until the end of our time together. I know now that I can pledge with this ring to be loving and faithful, in sickness and in health, but also in exploration and growth until death parts us.

Hand clasps! Hugs! Cameras! Everyone signed our witness certificate. Whoopee!

After a while, all of us trooped over to Barbara's apartment for a celebration featuring cake and champagne. For the cake, I had used an exotic recipe from one neighbor and the bundt pan of another, too shy to tell them what the event was going to be about.

Afterward

> March 3: The guests had gone, the cleanup chores were mostly done, and the hospitality bill was split. Finally—it was so hard for me to wait—we lay together again after a five-day lapse. My body and my life melds with Barbara's.

> I am still so much in love with this woman. How could this have lasted a whole year, this marvel? Is it slightly narcissistic? Maybe it is! We are so much alike—but also such different personalities. It is our great good luck.

18. Trajectories

Getting to this point

With rings on our fingers and more than a year of experience behind us, we remained amazed that we could have come together in this way.

Each of us pondered our own history. There was nothing romantic or intimate in our backgrounds but men, men, men. Husbands and lovers, short-term and long. Our sexual experiences with these men were satisfactory at the least and overwhelmingly rewarding at best.

The Women's Lib movement boiled up around us. We became aware of lesbians among our friends and colleagues and learned a little about their situations. I was approached tentatively by such women—about once per decade of my adult life, I realized now—but I was never attracted in that direction, though I have remained friends for many years with most of those good women.

Barb and I know only a little about the whole hard history of lesbian women during those coming-out years, mainly from books and occasional movies. We have no personal experience of the anguish of the girl who knows at a young age that she cannot respond sexually to guys and thus cannot happily walk the path society wants for her. Now, in twenty-first-century California, although we were nervous at first being public together, we were never scared, threatened, or reviled.

The Coming Out Stories collected by Julia Stanley and Susan Wolfe were poignant revelations for us. The women who came out while we were contentedly getting it on with men have smoothed and paved this new way for us, and we are fully aware and grateful. But even now as we engage each other with delight, we cannot use the expression lesbian for ourselves, precisely because we have not shared the hard history of persecution and struggle in the gay world. And we still know almost nothing about the lesbian community and its particular rich culture.

What I do know is that my lesbian friends of all these years are fine, fun-loving, grown-up women whom I am lucky to know and to whom I am committed. They helped to mark and clear the path that has led me to Barbara.

Perhaps becoming as whole, independent, and clear-thinking as possible lays the groundwork for a strong and growing partnership between any two people in old age. Preparing for a doctorate in education at age thirty-five, Barbara wrote her dissertation on how young high school teachers might be helped to develop the flexible, autonomous personalities best suited to bringing out the strengths inherent in teenagers. The humanistic description of human potential she offered in the middle of her thesis would readily match any desiderata posted on my wall at the same time. Paraphrased here are some prime items from her list of desirable human traits. The mature and growing human has

- free will;
- the capacity to evaluate past and present and to move forward into an uncertain future;
- self-expressiveness and the ability to engage authentically with others in I-Thou relationships;
- the urge to seek unifying rather than fragmenting understandings;
- the ability to relate the present to one's own past experience;
- a sense of personal adequacy and a positive self-concept;
- the ability to disclose and explain oneself in an authentic, non-defensive way;

- realistic expectations formed in the process of reflective self-awareness;

- awareness of the role of both perception and feeling in determining behavior;

- recognition of the [life-long] developmental stages of growth in cognitive, affective, and moral realms.

It stands to reason that Barbara and I are further along toward these goals than we were half our lives ago at age thirty-five. No wonder our relationship is proceeding so well!

That still leaves some of our specific milestones to explain. How did it happen that I was so ready for Barbara when she first sat down with me on that sofa? One answer suddenly came to me when I thanked my long-time friend and colleague, Marlane, for attending our ring ceremony. Here is part of the letter I ended up writing to her.

> Marlane, I also want to write down the insights I had early Saturday and spoke of during our little celebration about the role you have played in my life.
>
> Barbara and I have been talking in generalizations about how our way has been paved by women who have loved other

women before our time. We are so much in their (your) debt. But it is especially impressive for me to realize how you in particular have been present at important junctures in my life, helping to prepare the ground that would eventually and unexpectedly produce such a blossom and fruit as my love for Barbara Benham Tye.

- During those Monday morning staff sessions at work thirty-two years ago, over and over again you assured me that I could and would be an OK mother for my "wild" teenage daughter. (If I were not still OK, and if my daughter were not lately doing so well, could I have attracted or accepted Barbara?)

- In that scruffy cafe on the way to Tamalpais twenty-three years ago, you assured me that I would not be damned or struck by lightning if I lost my faith in a personal or tangible God. (My post-theist position is comfortable enough for my Barbara, who quietly calls herself an atheist.)

- By taking me (then more or less skinny) to that conference in Oakland, you taught me a great respect for grand women, great in body and in spirit. (Perhaps that helped to pave the way for me to adore Barbara's plush/lush body as I do.)

- In that amazing experience with hypnosis some fifteen years ago, you helped me consolidate my full acceptance of a death that would leave me without any kind of personal future in a heaven, reincarnated or anything like that—just restored to the holy ground of being. (This is a position which jibes more or less with Barbara's.)

- A little less than a year ago, I intuitively knew you should be the first to whom I would reveal my unexpected love for Barbara, asking for affirmation and guidance. Your first remark—"This doesn't make you lesbians, you know"—affirmed an understanding we hadn't yet reached but can testify to now. It set our feet on the right path.

- And now, your willingness to grow into friendship with Barbara and to share with her the (sacramental) role of final decider (aka health advocate) about my health care, should it come to that, is yet another blessing.

Dear friend, please accept my gratitude and respect for all these gifts. Please forgive any wistfulness our undeserved good luck might bring to you.

And please tell me when I can take you out to lunch to thank you in person and to debrief our happy ring ceremony on March 2.

Love, Elizabeth

Barbara talks about human trajectories and how they often intersect by mere chance. More is involved, though, than just ending up in the same place at the same time. The elements of need and/or readiness must also apply before two people on different trajectories connect as colleagues, teammates, friends, or lovers.

Our liaison would never have occurred if Barbara had not been widowed, left her old friends and family far behind, moved to this community, helped me so much with a professional problem, been of a size and shape that attracted me—on and on, the fluky, necessary components.

Our liaison would never have happened if I had not left friends and family, moved to this community, felt my children were finally pretty independent, lost some of the support I had been used to from a sister, gotten Barb's help with a difficult social problem, etc. These things just fell into place. My path suddenly intersected with Barbara's, and the road forward now is a single one and goes in the right direction for each of us.

Going forward

We think about how we want to move onward into our joint future. We need to remain our true selves, but making time for one another, for deep talk as well as for love making, has become top priority for us. It cuts into the kind of social life we had before, but sometimes we include other friends in our daily meetings. We each like seeing how the other interacts with friends and family. And we each visit on our own with special friends.

One of the easiest practices to drop if we are not careful is long-distance phone conversations with sisters (mine), brothers (hers), and friends (both) who live far away. I think my closest sister has mild feelings of jealousy about Barb, but she is so busy with her grandchildren that she hasn't much time to worry about me. She and I try to schedule phone dates, write them in our calendars, and then actually follow through—that's the hard part—so that we won't lose touch. Barbara and I don't want to lean too hard just upon one another.

Already, when Barbara goes out of town for some reason or when I go away myself, I find myself feeling lonely and missing her. These are new experiences for me after forty years of living alone, and they irritate me. *Am I not a strong and independent woman, after all?* And yet, other times, for hours at a time, when preoccupied with the task at hand or the people I am with, I give her nary a thought. I've still got work to do to get comfortable with these shifts of feeling.

We are pleased that our neighbors in this close retirement community also apparently give us no thought. (They didn't even notice our rings!) We are, after all, just like everyone else around here, indistinguishable, "the old lady with white hair." We have kept up our responsibilities and carried on as people knew us before, curtailing our obligations carefully so we leave no one in the lurch as we make time for one another.

Like our neighbors, our children and friends mostly seem to pay us no mind as well. Unless they want to express admiration! One young man the age of my grandchildren, hearing that I had a new "girlfriend," expressed admiration and delight that "there are old people around who can do something really new." Then he confessed his own polyamory to me—I think he meant that he lives (and sleeps) with at least two people in a mixed-gender circle.

The more settled we become, the more attention we can spare for others, including the world at large. Our happiness is in marked contrast to how much of the world lives, and we know ourselves to be unfairly fortunate. Sometimes this "heaven" is almost too much for me, and I read for respite about tough places and stricken people very far afield from here: a man in Afghanistan, a train trip in Russia, an evacuee in Sri Lanka, immigrants in Los Angeles—anything different from this marvelous and desirable life we are leading and loving. Doesn't sound rational, does it? Maybe it isn't, but it keeps a balance, protects my perspective on things.

Lately, I suffer the guilt of the survivor to a certain extent and worry that I should be doing more to "save the world" from disaster. It is climate change that threatens us the most, even more than the deterioration of democracy. Barbara shares my concern, but like others, we constantly shy away from thinking about it. We have been so preoccupied! Only recently have we begun to acknowledge the planetary threat and our responsibility to help avert it or adapt to it. I resolve that as soon as this book is finished, I'll get back to political advocacy.

19. Into the future

Death holds no terrors for me. In my view, heaven and hell are here on earth only. Reincarnation doesn't appeal to me because it presumes the continued existence of my own ego. Why would I want that? It is ego and consciousness of self that cause all the suffering in our lives, as far as I can see. Why wouldn't we be glad to give it up in the end, to return to the holy Whole from which birth separated us so long ago? To die, finally, is what we have been living for all this time.

Years ago, I wrote what I consider to be my best poem. I tried to express these views of life and death using metaphorical terms. At that time, I thought that Eros, the god of love and creativity, was beginning to release me to Thanatos, the god of death, and I was really happy about it.

Just One Day

Of all the long-lived days of my life,
there will be just the one
on which I die.

I will have given up

many delights by then,
many burdens and concerns
as well.

The two lover-gods of all my years
will accompany me. Eros
will finally release me from
the passion and creativity
he has required of me so long.
He'll help me shed
the multiple vestments
of the separate self so that
I am lovely and light when
Thanatos takes me in his arms
and carries me over
the threshold, like a bride,
into the radiant darkness.

But now, with this unexpected romance, Eros has
surged forward in my life again. Partnering Barbara, I
have this last complex and creative task to fulfill before
I can give myself over to Thanatos. He has receded
into the shadows. But he has promised me that he will
return.

All of us, men and women alike, who hook up
with a new partner late in life, stand knowingly under
a Damocles sword—under two such swords, in fact,
which may at any time fall upon our heads. The chances

of accident, illness, disability, or sudden death are far greater for us than for young lovers, and any hurt to one of us will greatly affect the other as well.

Happily, it is Barbara with whom I take this risk, not some man! In my conventional thinking, it is much preferred to face a future with a weakened woman than with a decimated man, especially one who is a hypochondriac, a blamer, or a complainer.

A strong woman, on the other hand, might stand up well to the challenges of being a patient. Early on, an emergency run to the hospital with Barbara one day, after a fall that cracked her eyebrow, was reassuring and decisive for me. In the ER that day, I saw that Barbara was stoic about the pain and inconvenience, appreciative of every helper, and positive about cooperating with the recovery plan. With this kind of patient, I knew I could go the distance.

In fact, instead of scaring us off, the possibility of hardship not very far down the road seems to deepen and enrich our relationship. Like others we talk to, we have appreciated in the past or now look forward to having the challenging experience of being an end-of-life caregiver. Barbara and I find that each of us envisions being the surviving spouse, anticipating it as an opportunity to rally strength and devotion on behalf of the other. Having spent many adult years alone, each of us is more confident about being the survivor than about being the frail and dependent one.

My mother deteriorated into dementia and paranoia in her last years, quite probably because of oxygen deprivation. I inherit the same vulnerable lungs and worry that dementia could overtake me, too. My worry is not for myself as much as it is for Barbara as my overseer and advocate. Dementia is always increasingly hard to deal with. There is supportive staff on site here, we can afford paid help for personal care, and I am not averse to dying in a skilled nursing facility or a residential hospice. But Barbara, if she is still here, will be much involved. I hope I can be as coherent until my dying day as were her husband and her mother, both of whom died at home under her care.

Living among people much older than we are gives us opportunity to observe the different ways in which people die. Barbara wrote in her journal about one:

> I must say a word about Joan, who phoned me today from her hospice room at Memorial Hospital. She thanked me again for offering rides for any resident(s) she really wants to see—to say goodbye to—but she and Joe [her husband] have agreed, no more visitors and no phone calls. She has stopped eating, I gather, and today the oxygen has been

withdrawn so that her body can take its own course.

I don't know why she picked me to reach out to, as we never got very close, but I am honored by it and am in awe of her courage. She's handling her dying process the way I hope to handle mine, in due course.

We were very interested and proud when another neighbor, having suffered debilitating heart disease for over a year at age ninety, took advantage of the new California End-of-Life-Options Act to choreograph the details of his own death: time, place, people with him, and so forth. His doctor and pharmacist helped him get the appropriate "cocktail" of medications. He died a few hours after he took them.

At this point, however, my own idea is just to stop eating when my life is no longer productive. I understand there are medications to suppress appetite. I think I would rather not control the exact time of my death. Fading away slowly seems like a good idea. But my ideas may change when the time comes.

It is interesting, possibly appalling, that we two committed ourselves to these unknown futures within a few weeks of falling in love. Fortunately, for over a year now, we have never wavered but instead have gotten increasingly confident about our ability to go the distance.

For me, this commitment plays a role in our decision not to live together. If we shared a home and I were to get ill, Barbara would be burdened by me all the time. It is important to me that in such a circumstance, she should have her own apartment as a retreat and a respite, her own safe space with her own treasured things and her own routines to buoy her up. And when I die, she should not be under pressure to move to a different, smaller living space, as sometimes happens in retirement communities. The same applies in reverse if she should reach her final illness before I do. For both of us, it is reassuring to know that whichever of us is the survivor will be surrounded by this close-knit, cooperative community where there will always be useful work to do and friendly people to share with.

In anticipation of these hard times ahead, we consciously pursue several practices now:

1. Laugh as often as possible.

2. Go for broke as far as sex is concerned, while the going is good.

3. Take in plays, concerts, short drives out of town, movies, visits with relatives. We want to read aloud to each other, listen to

music—and our community here provides many stimulating talks and events.

4. Regularly update our health and long-term care insurance policies, advance directives, HIPAA instructions, obituaries, wills, and trust agreements, and our communications about these things with our heirs and one another.

5. Learn all we can about hospice services, palliative care, the California End-of-Life Options Act, related pharmaceuticals, and similar topics.

We talk together and with our neighbors about whether we will accept surgery, chemotherapy, radiation, and all the rest as we get older and then really old. Maybe we will not. We know it cannot be decided theoretically, but at least we will have a good background of information when we make our case-by-case decisions.

Nowadays, there is more and more information in books and online about these matters. By far the best book we have encountered to date is Sallie Tisdale's *Advice for Future Corpses and those who love them.*

Blunt, practical, and hard-hitting, Tisdale "draws upon her many years of nursing, including ten years in palliative care." We talked it up and bought copies for friends and relatives. Barbara reviewed it for a local newsletter. Here are the prime points she made:

> Be prepared to encounter a lively treatment of topics such as *What is a "good" death? What happens to a dying person in the last months, weeks, and days? And how can caregivers and family members best be prepared to help?* Not by doing what *they* think should be done, but by doing—or not doing—what the dying person would like. *Pain control, palliative care, a dying person's decision to stop eating. Dying in a hospital versus dying at home?*
>
> One of my favorite chapters is the one on communicating effectively with a person who is engaged in the process of dying. Tisdale is clear: listening is the most important part. Give the person your full attention. Ask questions. Listen some more. Beware of "the urge to become parental under stress, to take charge and try to manage the situation. Taking charge protects you from having to feel helpless but may not be what the person really needs" (pp. 68-69).
>
> Exceptionally helpful, I feel, are Tisdale's tips for the caregiver on what *not* to say. Don't say: you're going to be fine. Don't make

promises or tell lies. Don't offer advice. Don't try to cheer the person up—it's disrespectful and shows lack of attention to the hard work that he or she is doing. Don't talk about your uncle who had the same disease and survived it.

Above all, one needs to remember that "what the person in the bed wants is all that counts." It's not about us, the survivors, our pain or our anxiety or our emotional needs. Somehow, we must set all our own baggage aside if we truly want to be helpful.

Barb and I have talked our way through the Tisdale book, learning lots and clarifying our own thoughts about how we want our last days to be lived out.

The emphasis in the book is about how to be a good caregiver. *How about being a good patient? Would I? Could I?* Barb and I realize that each of us would rather be the caregiver, even though that means we might be the one left alone in the end. *How will I ever give in to being out of control, helpless, ugly, and miserable?* I'd better go talk to someone ahead of me on this path who has experience with being a helpless patient.

Meanwhile, we are in our seventies with no fatal illnesses while we live in a community where the average age is eighty-five, and many are twenty years older than we are. So this death and dying talk is good preparation, but it may be many years away for us. We can get back to the idea of laughing as often as possible! And that we do, along with the others around us. Researchers have documented that many people, especially women, find their sixties and seventies to be the happiest decades of their lives. Add in a little unexpected romance, and you are on top of the world!

Now that we have spent a year together, deeply engrossed in figuring out how to pursue and promote this relationship within the family, faith, and friend circles around us, we have gotten increasingly clear that it is appropriate to put into a book some of the things we have learned. Yes, we are *under a leading* to write about all this for publication.

"See a need and fill it!" There is not enough in print about how female lovers, including old ones, share their bodies and their lives; it was not safe to print this kind of thing until recently. Loving sex should be celebrated, and the world needs more explicit love poems for women together. New varieties of marriage are worth exploring. Pansexuality and androgyny are in the public eye these days, and we have a unique angle to share on both.

I worry about being too explicit and offending or embarrassing people, especially our siblings and children. But so far, they all encourage us to go ahead with it. So here we go.

We do have a few other plans and projects ahead, too. Having already traveled and lived in far parts of the world, we are not likely to leave this country again. (Air travel contributes substantially to climate change.) But we do think it will be healthy to take at least one weekend per quarter away from home. Sometimes it will be a sort of honeymoon weekend, sometimes a workshop or communal retreat. Sometimes it will involve our siblings or offspring. The two of us will celebrate our birthdays and our several anniversaries together, and sometimes one of us will go off on an expedition alone or with friends and family.

I am likely to work on another book of poems and, with my siblings, on a volume called *Boardman Family Stories Volume II*. (We wrote up childhood stories in *Volume I* some ten years back.)

Barbara is continuing to work on an historical novel about a distant relative from the early 1900s, definitely a liberated and androgynous woman. As a single woman traveling alone, Gertrude Benham climbed many of the most challenging mountains in the world and walked vast distances on every continent except Antarctica and Australia.

Our ongoing challenges include our tendency to dither over little decisions because we each want to defer to the preferences of the other. We are attentive also to the question of pace: Elizabeth's "engines idle high" while Barb's are "slow to tick over." Usually, though, we like how these traits balance out between the two of us.

I am pondering whether to call Barbara the love of my life. I have had a lot of loves in my life. For a while, I gave that title to the person who wrapped and ripped my heart the most: my daughter, as she struggled her traumatic way to adulthood. Best love doesn't necessarily have anything to do with romance or sex.

Now it is different. "Barbara, you're the one," I whisper to her. I mean the partner I gave up waiting for, never imagined finding at all, certainly not in another woman. It is not because of our deeply bonding sexual encounters that she is so special to me. It is because we are so compatible in social and cultural terms. She is a mature, androgynous woman, emotionally healthy, willing and able to share the vicissitudes of life. Our paths have unexpectedly brought us together in a most satisfactory way. Are there rough patches ahead? Most certainly. Are we scared? Not really. Whatever works, right? This is working wonderfully well.

About the author

This whole book having been about the author, it remains only to add that her earlier books, available on Amazon, also arose out of personal experience. In addition to two volumes of poetry, Elizabeth Boardman has written about taking a leading role in a Quaker congregation for several years, working in the Tenderloin of San Francisco, participating in an anti-war peace team in Iraq, and accompanying a brother during the last weeks of his life. She credits history professors at Harvard for teaching her to write.

CPSIA information can be obtained
at www.ICGtesting.com
Printed in the USA
BVHW081018201222
654624BV00018B/926